NIGELLA EXPRESS

Also by Nigella Lawson

HOW TO EAT
THE PLEASURES AND PRINCIPLES OF GOOD FOOD

HOW TO BE A DOMESTIC GODDESS
BAKING AND THE ART OF COMFORT COOKING

NIGELLA BITES

FOREVER SUMMER

FEAST
FOOD THAT CELEBRATES LIFE

NIGELLA EXPRESS

GOOD FOOD FAST · GOOD FOOD FAST · GOOD FOOD FAST

NIGELLA LAWSON

PHOTOGRAPHS BY LIS PARSONS

Chatto & Windus
LONDON

Published by Chatto & Windus 2009

13

Copyright © Nigella Lawson 2007
Photographs copyright © Lis Parsons 2007

Nigella Lawson has asserted her right under the Copyright, Designs
and Patents Act 1988 to be identified as the author of this work

First published in Great Britain in 2007 by
Chatto & Windus
Random House, 20 Vauxhall Bridge Road,
London SW1V 2SA

www.rbooks.co.uk

Addresses for companies within The Random House Group Limited
can be found at: www.randomhouse.co.uk/offices.htm

The Random House Group Limited Reg. No. 954009

A CIP catalogue record for this book
is available from the British Library

ISBN 9780701181840

Design and Art Direction: Caz Hildebrand
Cookery Assistant: Hettie Potter
Editorial Assistant: Zoe Wales
Props: Fiona Golfar & Rose Murray
Layout/Design: Julie Martin
Illustrations: Colin Frewin/West One Arts, Here Design
Index: Vicki Robinson

The Random House Group Limited supports The Forest Stewardship Council(FSC),the leading
international forest certification organization. All our titles that are printed on Greenpeace
approved FSC certified paper carry the FSC logo. Our paper procurement policy can
be found at www.rbooks.co.uk/environment

Printed and bound by C&C Offset Printing Co., Ltd., China

CONTENTS

INTRODUCTION

This is, as the title makes clear, a book about fast food, but it is a book about fast food for those who love eating. Perhaps that's self-evident: how could I write any other sort? But I start with this premise because so much is written about the need to reduce the time we must spend cooking it's as if the kitchen were a hateful place, almost an unsafe place, and that it must be only reasonable for us to avoid it. I love food, I adore being in the kitchen and I am happy to cook. But here's the problem: the day doesn't have enough gaps in it for me to do much shopping and the evening — what with the battles over homework, the still unchecked-off list of things I was meant to do, the calls I was supposed to return — doesn't yield much time to cook. But I must eat, and I must eat well — or else what is the point of it all? And then there are the people who need to be fed. I don't mention them grudgingly, either. I love to feed people, and rare is the person who comes into my home and leaves without a foil parcel of something from the kitchen.

I have had to adapt. I manage to have a fridge full of food and a life rich in the expectation of dinner but within the confines of a timetable that is disorganized, busy, full of things I want to do as well as things I don't want to do — though sometimes I'm so tired I can't tell the difference. In short, I have a normal life, the sort we all share. To be sure, I can occasionally find the odd weekend or rainy afternoon when I am able to lose myself in an afternoon's stirring, chopping, kneading or general pursuit of unhurried cooking, but for the most part, I am either in a hurry or in some state of psycho-fizz or obligation-overload and food has to be fitted in.

Even if I might never have thought that a book of fast food recipes would be the natural one for me to write, it has been both

pleasurable and easy. After all, the recipes are already there. For this is the food I do eat, day in day out. I don't know if I have quite spelt out my food obsessiveness before, but it's the case that I take notes of every thing I cook (even if the notes are sometimes hard to read later) and I keep a digital camera in the kitchen to record each finished dish, if not for posterity, for my own greedy archives. In a way, then, this book has written itself. This is just as well, since I left myself barely enough time to write it. My sister, Horatia, said I was like Wallace and Gromit, laying down the tracks just in time for the train to ride over them; and although it's been a bit hairy at times, it does, however, seem entirely fitting for a book called *Nigella Express*.

I feel, though, that I must emphasize this: cooking is only one part of the exercise; the shopping and planning can be the most stressful parts. I have tried to keep the ingredients lists as short as possible and, although I haven't excluded all recondite items from them, I try to make sure any shopping trip pays for itself, timewise. That's to say, if I ask you (or myself) to buy something for one recipe, I try to supply other outings for it. But avoiding the recherché or unfamiliar wouldn't be the answer, in any case: after all, there is no way, however basic the supplies required, that shopping can be dispensed with. Eggs and bacon don't magically appear in the kitchen: they need to be shopped for just as coconut milk or wasabi does. I make this embarrassingly obvious point, because I think we all need reminding of it.

It's not, however, for me to tell you how to plan your shopping or order your storecupboard. I do much of my shopping on the internet (too much, some would say), go to specialist stores when I find the time (for me that's fun, not duty), and have the odd turn around the supermarket. In the occasional recipe, where I've thought it might be helpful, I've noted an online stockist for an ingredient that could be harder for you to source locally.

I've also been quite strict with myself. I can't – couldn't possibly – eradicate all witter from my writing life, but I have tried to restrict the babble to the introduction to each recipe and have then given the method in a number of short, precise steps. This is to make sure you never have to turn a page to continue a recipe and to help every step read as clearly as it can. There isn't a recipe in here that isn't gloriously simple to cook, and I wanted to make that immediately evident on the page.

I could go on, but in the interest of brevity and the Express spirit, it seems only right to cut straight to the chase. The recipes that follow are not simply quick to cook, they attempt to make the whole of your cooking life – and as a consequence all of your life – easier. They are arranged in chapters, but please don't feel confined by these. Read, browse, sample, fiddle about as you see fit. As in cooking, so in life: we muddle through as best we can and this is what *Nigella Express* is all about.

NOTE FOR THE READER

- ALL EGGS ARE LARGE, ORGANIC
- ALL BUTTER IS UNSALTED
- ALL HERBS ARE FRESH, UNLESS STATED
- ALL CHOCOLATE IS DARK (MIN. 70% COCOA SOLIDS), UNLESS STATED
- SEE PAGE 353 FOR INFORMATION ABOUT INFUSED OILS

Most days, I approach cooking supper with less than absolute perkiness. This is never because I can't face it or even that I resent it, but because, at the end of a long, working day, and after I have wrestled with children's homework and other domestic demands, and feel that I am nothing more than the sum of my impatience and tetchy exhaustion, I just can't even think of what there might be to cook.

Actually, the cooking itself is the least of it, and this is not just because the kitchen is a place of sanctuary for me. Now, planning, shopping, deciding: these are the real drainers. I sometimes think how much easier things were in my grandmother's day. She had a schedule, and an unchanging one. Without looking at a diary, I could know what day of the week it was by what I was given for dinner. Of course, we are more adventurous these days and would not wish to inflict that tedium on our children. But a little of that Ordnung is desirable. In fact, I think it can lead to more variation rather than less. I don't like to own up to how often my children get pasta with pesto or meat sauce for supper because I am accustomed to life as a free spirit in the kitchen.

So now I try, while writing my shopping lists, to make sure that I am a little more repetitive than I once might have liked. Luckily, I begin to see that repetition, too, has its virtues. I know, at least, that I can get supper on the table without going shopping afresh every day. I don't follow the recipes below enormously rigorously; that's to say I certainly deviate, both in the regularity with which they appear and the irregularity with which I follow them. I am not good at authority, even when that authority is my own.

Still, I have one rule and it's simple enough to adhere to: it's never worth cooking anything for supper unless it can stand on equal footing with one of life's great and simplest gastro-delights: boiled egg on toast (the best Italian eggs, soft boiled, rapidly peeled and squished on thick sourdough or rye toast). Of course, I don't want that every day, but nor do I want to settle for anything less. If it can't measure up to that, I don't want to eat it. However little time or effort I can expend on the day's supper, I have to know it will deliver nothing less than pure pleasure. The recipes that follow satisfy that most necessary of edicts.

SMOKED COD AND CANNELLINI

Of all my reliable standbys, this is one of the speediest. Of course there's more to it. I'm too greedy to settle for mere efficiency. I first made this with some smoked haddock which I'd been thinking of using for a kedgeree, but I ran out of steam – and time. My thinking was that replacing the starch of the rice with the starch of some cannellini beans would work. It did. Indeed, it worked so well, I can now never be without some canned cannellini in the cupboard.

Inspiration doesn't tell the whole story, as the dish that follows bears no relation at all to kedgeree, being rather more Italianate than Anglo-Indian in its flavour. The spontaneity of end-of-the-day cooking means – whatever my best intentions – that this is, in culinary terms, *sui generis*.

But then I take the view that most of the best things in life are happy accidents.

350g smoked cod (or haddock) fillets
small sprig parsley, including stalks
2 bay leaves
1 teaspoon peppercorns
1 celery stalk
375ml water
80ml white wine
2 x 410g cans cannellini beans

60–125ml fish-cooking liquid (see 3, below)
2 x 15ml tablespoons extra virgin olive oil
2 x 15ml tablespoons chopped parsley
1 x 15ml tablespoon chopped fresh chives (optional)
salt and pepper to taste

1 Lay the fish fillets in a large frying pan with the sprig of parsley, bay leaves, peppercorns and celery stalk. Pour in the water and wine and bring to the boil.

2 Cover the pan with foil and simmer the fish in the poaching liquid for 3–5 minutes, depending on the thickness of the fish. Take off the heat and remove the fish, wrapping the pieces in foil to keep warm.

3 Tip out all but about 60ml of the poaching liquid from the pan. (The amount depends on the depth of your pan. You will need just enough to warm through the beans.)

4 Drain the canned beans, rinsing them in a sieve or colander to get rid of any gloopiness, and add to the pan. Warm them in the poaching liquid for about 3 minutes.

5 Turn off the heat and place the fish on top of the beans in the pan. Add the oil, most of the parsley and the chives, if you're using them, stirring everything together and breaking up the fish as you go.

6 Check the seasoning and turn out into a couple of bowls or onto plates, sprinkle with a last bit of parsley and eat, with relish.

Serves 2

I love the tangy fire of Thai cooking; I love equally the traditional English partnership of lamb with redcurrant and mint. I just happened, one day, because of what I had in the kitchen, to bring the two together. Consider it an ovine reworking of those hot and sour beef salads of south east Asia. A lamb loin, sometimes described as the eye of the saddle, is the fleshy component, though any lean cut of lamb would do. Redcurrant jelly stands in for the sweetness of jaggery or palm sugar and I use rice vinegar (always to hand in my store cupboard) instead of lime juice. I am not married to someone who would normally regard a salad as a treat for supper, but my husband loves this – and doesn't even notice it is a salad.

It is also a useful recipe to have up your sleeve for a starter on days when dining seems to require one. I try to keep those days – or nights – to a minimum, or to when I'm in a restaurant.

2 teaspoons garlic oil
1 lamb loin, approx. 250g
1 packet (approx. 180g) salad leaves
3 x 15ml tablespoons chopped mint

FOR THE DRESSING
2 x 15ml tablespoons fish sauce (nam pla)

1 x 15ml tablespoon redcurrant jelly
2 x 15ml tablespoons rice vinegar
1 teaspoon soy sauce
1 red chilli, deseeded and finely chopped, or $^1/_4$ teaspoon crushed chillies
1 spring onion, finely sliced

1   Heat the oil in a heavy-based pan, and cook the lamb for 5 minutes on one side, and then turn it over and cook for another $2^1/_2$ minutes on the other.

2   Wrap the meat in foil, making a baggy but tightly sealed parcel, and let it rest for about 5 minutes.

3   In a medium-sized bowl, whisk together the dressing ingredients.

4   Open the foil parcel, and empty the meat juices into the dressing. Cut the lamb into very fine slices or strips and add them too; the acid in the dressing will "cook" the lamb a little more while it steeps. If the meat is not rare, I'd leave it for just a short time, but for a longer time if it seems undercooked. You want it still gorgeously pink to sit on its salad.

5   Divide the salad leaves between 2 (or 4) plates and then arrange the soused lamb with the dressing over each one. Finally scatter the chopped mint on top.

Serves 2 as a main course; 4 as a starter

Salmon Escalopes with Watercress, Sugar-Snap Peas and Avocado

This is an ideal recipe for those days when you're as squeezed for time to shop as to cook: you just rush into the supermarket at lunch or on the way home, snatch a few packets, and rush out again.

"Wok oil" is how the oil I like to use here comes labelled: it contains vegetable oil, sesame oil, ginger and garlic; but garlic oil, chilli oil or, indeed, just oil-oil would be fine.

2 thin-cut salmon steaks or escalopes, approx. 125g each
2 x 15ml tablespoons rice vinegar
1 teaspoon sugar
1/2 teaspoon Maldon salt or
1/4 teaspoon table salt

2 x 15ml tablespoons wok oil
100g watercress
100g miniature sugar-snap peas
1 small ripe avocado

1 Heat a heavy-based, non-stick frying pan and, when hot, cook the salmon steaks or escalopes for about a minute a side. Remove to a couple of dinner plates.

2 Whisk the rice vinegar, sugar, salt and wok oil together and drizzle each salmon steak with about a teaspoon each, and then set the rest aside for a moment.

3 Divide the watercress and sugar-snaps between each plate. Halve the avocado, remove the stone and, using a teaspoon, gouge out the avocado flesh, dropping the pieces as you go in among the tangle of watercress and sugar-snaps.

4 Pour the remaining dressing over each salad and serve immediately.

Serves 2

MUSTARD PORK CHOPS

I love the old French favourites, the sorts that evoke not the supercilious waiter and theatrically-removed silvered dome of the big-name restaurants, but rather the small town bistro, all warm wood and rough red.

This is possibly the easiest route to a proper, filling and yet strangely delicate dinner. The pork is cooked for just enough time to take away any pinkness but ensure tenderness within, and is gloriously scorched without. The mustard, cider and cream add comfort and piquancy.

To soak up the juices, and to act as a fantastically quicktime potato substitute, I serve up gnocchi alongside. You could always add a little lemony fennel, sliced thinly, or a green salad if you're in the mood.

> 2 pork chops, approx. 450g total
> 2 teaspoons garlic oil
> 125ml cider
> 1 x 15ml tablespoon grainy mustard
> 75ml double cream

1   Cut the fat or rind off the chops, and then bash them briefly but brutally with a rolling pin between two pieces of clingfilm to make them thinner.

2   Heat the oil in a heavy-based pan and cook the chops over a moderately high heat for about 5 minutes a side. Remove them to a warmed plate.

3   Pour the cider into the pan, still over the heat, to de-glaze the pan. Let it bubble away for a minute or so, then add the mustard and stir in the cream.

4   Let the sauce continue cooking for a few minutes before pouring over each plated pork chop. If you're having gnocchi with it, make sure you turn them in the pan to absorb any spare juices before adding them to your plates.

Serves 2

Turkey Fillets with Anchovy, Gherkin and Dill

I have long been an excitable fan of turkey, that's to say the familiar festive roast turkey, but I have come only recently to appreciate the blander, leaner cuts that line our supermarkets' refrigerated shelves. Do I sound sneering? Force of habit, perhaps. I have always resisted the sort of meat that is prized almost exclusively for its low fat content (what a thing to do, to like food for what it lacks), but I've found myself cooking with turkey pieces more and more. Not least, I like the contrast of its mild meat to sharp, pungent flavourings, the sort of flavourings that live by my hob and lend themselves very handsomely to lazy evening cooking.

The saltiness of the anchovies and the sharpness of the gherkins give the timid turkey real bite here, and I love the Germanic sprinkling of dill. I tend to eat this with something plain: rice from the rice cooker or some steamed tiny new potatoes or a vast plate of broccoli. The broccoli (in this case fabulous sprouting purple broccoli) needs no more than some butter or oil, but if you feel like going all out (relatively speaking), try the Mustard Caper Sauce that follows. The recipe was given to me by the book's designer, Caz Hildebrand, and hence is known, *chez moi*, as Caz's Capers.

5 anchovy fillets

2 x 15ml tablespoons olive oil

3 small turkey breast fillets (approx. 400g total weight), beaten as thinly as possible, each fillet then cut in half

2 x 15ml tablespoons vermouth

2 gherkins, finely chopped

2 x 15ml tablespoons chopped fresh dill

1 Heat the anchovy fillets and oil in a large, heavy-based frying pan, stirring with a wooden spoon until the fillets begin to melt in the pan.

2 Flash-fry the turkey in the same pan, cooking for a couple of minutes each side. Remove the meat to a warm serving plate.

3 Add the vermouth and chopped gherkins, and let the liquid reduce and sizzle for a minute or so.

4 Pour over the plated turkey and sprinkle with the chopped dill.

Serves 4

MUSTARD CAPER SAUCE FOR BROCCOLI

75g butter
2 teaspoons Dijon mustard

juice of $\frac{1}{2}$ lemon
2 x 15ml tablespoons capers

1 Put the butter, mustard and lemon juice into a pan over a medium heat.

2 As the butter melts, whisk all the ingredients together and then add the capers.

3 Pour the emulsified sauce over your cooked and drained purple sprouting broccoli and serve.

Makes enough to dress about 250–500g broccoli

RED PRAWN AND MANGO CURRY

This is one of the easiest suppers to make, but somehow, however much I know this, it always surprises me. Not in the cooking, so much as in the eating: I can't believe, each time anew, how deep and textured and full-throttle, in a sweet, comforting way, this tastes, when all I've done is a bit of shopping and some light stirring.

Obviously it helps if you can use some of the convenience stuff I list below: the ready-peeled, cubed squash and sweet potato, and the mango I get at the supermarket make this a breeze. But if you can't find them, no matter: add a few drained canned chick-peas and perhaps, for a sour-sweet edge, some pineapple that's been in its own juice, not syrup. And if you're not familiar with wok oil, see page 353. As for the coconut milk, I often use the whole can rather than the mere half below; it really depends on whether I feel like eating out of a deep bowl, soupily, or a shallow one. To go with it, I suggest either plain rice or some plain wide rice noodles cooked according to packet instructions (all of about 2 minutes) and tossed in some toasted chopped unsalted peanuts.

If you have some fresh prawns, so much the better, but I stipulate frozen ones below since I regularly keep them in the freezer for an evening when I feel like eating gorgeously with very little forethought.

1 x 15ml tablespoon wok oil	2 teaspoons fish sauce (nam pla)
1 spring onion, finely sliced	1 x 350g packet butternut and sweet
1^1/$_2$ x 15ml tablespoons red Thai	potato cubes
curry paste (or according to taste)	1 x 200g packet frozen king prawns
^{1}/$_2$ x 400ml can coconut milk, to	1 teaspoon lime juice
give 200ml	150g mango cubes, diced
250ml chicken stock (made from	3–4 x 15ml tablespoons chopped fresh
concentrate)	coriander

1 Heat the wok oil in a large, heavy-based frying pan, and fry the sliced spring onion for a minute, then add the curry paste.

2 Whisk in the coconut milk, chicken stock and fish sauce and bring to the boil.

3 Tip in the butternut squash and sweet potato cubes and simmer, partially covered, for about 15 minutes, or until tender.

4 Drain the prawns under running water to remove excess ice and tumble them in to the pan, letting the sauce come back to the boil. When it does, add the lime juice and diced mango and cook for another minute or so until the prawns are cooked through.

5 Sprinkle with the chopped coriander as you serve over plain rice or wide rice noodles, or even both.

Serves 2–4, depending on how hungry you are and whether you're expecting to eat anything else at supper

QUICK CALAMARI WITH GARLIC MAYONNAISE

Strange though it might sound, this is another of my supper-standbys. I keep the frozen squid in the deep freeze, taking it out in the morning at breakfast to let it thaw in time for the evening's meal. I prefer to eat a massive amount of this, and nothing else, rather than have it more meanly as a starter, unless I'm expecting company, in which case it can happily stretch to four people, ready to dunk each crisp piece of squid into the garlic mayonnaise over pre-dinner drinks.

250ml groundnut oil, or as needed depending on size of pan
500g frozen squid (tubes and tentacles)
2 x 15ml tablespoons cornflour
4 x 15ml tablespoons semolina
2 teaspoons Old Bay seasoning (or use 1 teaspoon salt and 1 teaspoon paprika)

FOR THE GARLIC MAYONNAISE
$^1/_2$ clove garlic
100g best-quality mayonnaise (preferably organic)

1 Heat the oil in a smallish saucepan and, while it's left to warm up, cut the thawed squid into 1cm rings.

2 Put the cornflour, semolina and seasoning into a plastic freezer bag.

3 Add the squid rings and tentacles and then toss to coat.

4 When the oil is hot enough, which is when it sizzles up fiercely when you drop in a small cube of bread, fry the squid in batches to get the most golden crunchiness. A couple of minutes per batch is all you should need.

5 Grate or crush the garlic into the mayonnaise, stir to mix, and then serve alongside the fried squid.

Serves 2 as a main course, 4 as a starter

NAAN PIZZA

At times when I'm pretending to indulge the children, but am really too exhausted to cook, I order in takeout pizza. But actually this naan pizza is my preferred option. I can eat a whole pizza in its box and always regret it afterwards. This one is not much harder to cook than making a phone call and I feel much happier for it. I've given my topping of preference; feel free to play about to make your own. All I feel strongly is that while shop-bought pizza bases are vile, packet naans, when heated, are not.

1 shop-bought naan
2 teaspoons tomato pulp (chopped and sieved tomatoes) from a jar (or other tomato sauce)
70g drained mixed mushrooms antipasto from a jar
75g fontina cheese, roughly chopped
3 stalks thyme

1 Preheat the oven to 220°C/gas mark 7. Lay the naan on a lined baking sheet.

2 Spread the tomato pulp or sauce over the naan, then tumble the drained mushrooms on top and sprinkle with the chopped cheese, before finally strewing with the thyme leaves stripped from the stalks.

3 Cook in the oven for about 5 minutes, by which time the cheese should be bubbling and melted. Be careful not to burn your mouth.

Serves 1

ROAST POUSSIN AND SWEET POTATOES

This is my almost regular as clockwork Saturday night supper. I find it enormously easy and relaxing to make since all I do is go downstairs, put everything in the oven, and then go back up to Saturday evening TV in bed until it's ready – and then, frankly, back again.

If I cook the poussins in the same pan as the sweet potatoes, I cut a couple of slices of bread and put one underneath each bird in the tin to absorb the juices and stop them from seeping into the sweet potatoes, which, in turn, would prevent them from crisping and browning. But, more often than not, I dispense with the bread (you can imagine how good it tastes later though) and just get two disposable foil roasting trays about the size of brownie tins. I put the poussins in one tray and the sweet potatoes in another and reunite them on the plate with a little watercress and a squirt of lime juice later.

I must have English mustard with this. I know it's a weakness, but not one I'm willing to renounce.

2 poussins
2 x 15ml tablespoons garlic oil or
    wok oil
1 sweet potato, approx. 500g
$^1/_4$ teaspoon ground cumin

$^1/_4$ teaspoon ground cinnamon
1–2 bunches watercress
salt and pepper to taste
good squirt of lime juice

1 Preheat the oven to 220°C/gas mark 7. Put the birds into a small baking tin or foil tray, and pour 1 tablespoon of oil over them.

2 Cut the unpeeled sweet potatoes into 5cm cubes and put them into another smallish baking tin or foil tray.

3 Pour the remaining tablespoon of oil over the potatoes, sprinkle the spices on top, and then shake the tin to toss everything together.

4 Cook both the poussins and sweet potatoes in the hot oven for 45 minutes.

5 Put each poussin on a plate, with a tangle of watercress and the sweet potatoes alongside. Sprinkle with salt (I prefer Maldon) and pepper to taste, spritz with lime juice, and go to it!

Serves 2

CARAMEL CROISSANT PUDDING

I always think that some of the best recipes come from the thrifty refusal to throw any-thing away. Certainly, I made this one Monday evening because I had two stale croissants left over from the weekend and just knew they could be put to good use. Now, adding cream and bourbon is probably a lot less thrifty than throwing some stale bread away in the first place, but this is such a fabulous pudding that I now think it should be every Monday night's supper. And I mean supper: with something this substantial, you certain-ly need eat nothing beforehand. Though I admit a small crunchy salad may not be a bad idea first.

Oh, and if you don't have any bourbon in the house, first may I say, please con-sider it, and second, replace it, rather, with rum; Scotch whisky may seem the obvious substitute but it would be the wrong one I feel.

2 stale croissants	125ml full-fat milk
100g caster sugar	2 x 15ml tablespoons bourbon
2 x 15ml tablespoons water	2 eggs, beaten
125ml double cream	

1 Preheat the oven to 180°C/gas mark 4.

2 Tear the croissants into pieces and put in a small gratin dish; I use a cast iron oval one with a capacity of about 500ml for this.

3 Put the caster sugar and water into a saucepan, and swirl around to help dissolve the sugar before putting the saucepan on the hob over a medium to high heat.

4 Caramelize the sugar and water mixture by letting it bubble away, without stirring, until it all turns a deep amber colour; this will take 3–5 minutes. Keep looking but don't be too timid.

5 Turn heat down to low and add the cream – ignoring all spluttering – and, whisking away, the milk and bourbon. Any solid toffee that forms in the pan will dissolve easily if you keep whisking over low heat. Take off the heat and, still whisking, add the beaten eggs. Pour the caramel bourbon custard over the croissants and leave to steep for 10 minutes if the croissants are very stale.

6 Place in the oven for 20 minutes and prepare to swoon.

Serves 2 greedy people

Rhubarb and Custard Gelato

There is no variation on rhubarb and custard I don't love, and this is probably one of the easiest to make. You buy some good-quality, eggy vanilla ice cream and then make this compote – it's very quick, and gorgeous poured warm over the ice cream, with the rest chilled in the fridge and eaten with yogurt for breakfast.

500g untrimmed rhubarb
150g caster sugar
2 x 15ml tablespoons best-quality vanilla extract

TO SERVE
few scoops of ice cream (enough for 2 people)

1   Cut the rhubarb into 5mm slices, discarding the leaves and tough ends.

2   Put the rhubarb, caster sugar and vanilla extract into a saucepan and bring to the boil, stirring as the pan heats up, to help dissolve the sugar.

3   Partially cover the pan and simmer for about 3 minutes, then uncover completely and cook for another couple of minutes, or until the rhubarb is soft, and melting into the pink syrup, though still keeping its shape – just.

4   Pour into a jug and leave to cool a little, before pouring over the ice cream.

Makes approx. 500ml compote, enough for a good 6 portions, but feel happy to use as much as you like

BUTTERSCOTCH FRUIT FONDUE

If ever you've – lazily, guiltily – bought ready-peeled, sliced, cubed fruit from the super-market, and then wondered why you bothered, when you get home to discover the fruit is brightly hued but dimly flavoured, this is the solution. Anything, frankly, dunked into butterscotch sauce tastes good, and this is a fabulous everyday or even party pudding.

I own up, the fruit in the picture did come out of a cellophane box – the mango ready cubed, the melon ready sliced – but mostly I make this for the children, using bananas and pears I have managed to peel and slice myself. The strawberries you don't even need to hull: their stalks are useful to lower the berries into the molten fondue.

I give everyone – here just the two of us – a little cup of fondue for their own individual dipping. It does mean you make more sauce than is needed, but gets round the shared spit and saliva issue. Or you could make half the amount and pour over a cubed mix of pineapple, papaya and mango.

Either way, you don't want the butterscotch fondue too fiercely hot, not least because it will be too runny. If you make it before you sit down to eat, it should be just about perfect by the time you reach pudding. I am also pretty keen on this cold, spooned straight from the cup.

45g light muscovado sugar
2 x 15ml tablespoons caster sugar
150g golden syrup
30g butter

125ml double cream
splash of vanilla extract
approx. 350g cut fruit

1 Melt the sugars, syrup and butter in a saucepan and boil for 5 minutes.

2 Add the cream and vanilla extract, stirring together, and then take off the heat.

3 Divide the sauce between two cups or small bowls, and then arrange the fruit on two saucers or on a plate, as you see fit.

Serves 2

WORKDAY WINNERS

There are few things so likely to put a strain on the working day as knowing you've got people coming over for supper a few minutes after you've walked through the front door, with barely time to take your coat off. I don't wish to sound negative. I do, it's true, have a tendency towards hermit-like cocooning, especially in the winter, but I also love to be in a room full of friends in the evening. And, now I think about it, it is mainly during the week that I have friends over for supper. Weekends can get taken over by my children's social life, so there really isn't time for my own. But that suits me. One of the good things about a midweek supper party is that no one expects the grand treatment. And I always, always prefer the mood to be informal.

So, make life easier on yourself by dispensing with a starter. I know I've said this before, but it bears repetition. It's not just that you don't want the extra cooking, but neither do you want an extra course's worth of washing up. And I don't think you want dinner to be an overlong affair. It may not sound hospitable, but who wants a really late night in the middle of the working week?

Only have a starter if it makes life easier for you. Sometimes it can help to have some food for people to pick at over a drink or two: it means you can get on with putting supper together calmly, and it keeps everyone happy. I also think sometimes it makes sense to balance the amount of food you have to put on the table. So, if you offer a first course, maybe you can provide just a salad with the main course, and no potatoes – that sort of thing. Sometimes I use a bit of starter action to make me feel less guilty about giving everyone roast chicken *again*. And you don't actually have to cook the starter: a few bits and pieces thrown together is all you need – like the Prawns with Maryam Zaira Sauce or Crab and Avocado Salad below, for obvious example.

You can take the lack of effort further, without feeling bad about it at all. A bit of judicious – and pleasurable if you're lucky – shopping and you don't have to do a thing. I buy some salame, uncut and still in sausage form, as well as some sliced, and arrange them with a knife or two on a wooden board. Parmesan, bought in a wedge and then cut into crumbly hunks is another labour-light way of going about feeding people when they arrive. Slightly higher up the effort scale, but only a tiny bit, is to buy frozen edamame beans from a store that sells Japanese foodstuffs. These are soybeans in the pod, which you boil for about 5 minutes from frozen and then sprinkle lavishly if unfashionably with rock salt before podding them and then popping their jade beans into the mouth, while still warm.

Buy a tub of hummus, mix it with half its volume of Greek yogurt, stir in a little ground cumin and grated lemon zest, then drizzle with olive oil, scatter with some pomegranate seeds and serve with breadsticks or sliced pitta. Or buy a good tub of lemony (preferably organic) mayonnaise and grate in a little garlic and set an array of raw vegetables on the table to dip into it. If you can't face chopping vegetables, then go heavy on sugar-snaps instead.

Above all, be relaxed. I know it's always an irritating injunction, but this should be a supper with friends, around a table, with you able to enjoy them. Food always helps, but even when a dinner's gone wrong, you can still have a great evening. And once you accept that mistakes in the kitchen don't need to matter, you're less likely to make them in the first place. Anyway, none of the recipes that follow should give either the novice or the merely tired any cause for culinary, or other, concern.

PRAWNS WITH MARYAM ZAIRA SAUCE

OK, so this is the idea: sauce Marie Rose goes Moroccan. Instead of the usual tomato ketchup (well, be honest), I dollop in some good shop-bought harissa. It works wonderfully, and the honey makes up for the sugar you lack by giving up the Heinz. Be careful when you buy harissa, though, as not only does it vary enormously in strength but also some jars that bear the name are not really harissa but a paste made red with beetroot and carrot. Check the back of the tub for ingredients. I used a gorgeously mild harissa here, a rose harissa, that I find poetically desirable. But start with a small amount of the harissa you've got before working up to the amount I have stipulated below.

I love prawns with their shells still on; a bit of DIY at the table always seems to help the atmosphere. But if you hate mess and can't bear the sight of seeing people dropping shells all over the place, then simply buy peeled prawns instead.

500g cooked prawns with shell on

FOR THE SAUCE
200g good-quality shop-bought mayonnaise, preferably organic
50g harissa
1 teaspoon lime juice
1 teaspoon honey

1 Mix together all the sauce ingredients, and put into a bowl suitable for dipping.

2 Arrange the prawns on a plate for people to pluck, peel and dip into the sauce, making sure you have enough in the way of plates or saucers dotted about the place for detritus.

Serves 4–6 as a starter

CRAB AND AVOCADO SALAD WITH JAPANESE DRESSING

This is another one of those salads that my husband doesn't notice is a salad and that we eat fairly often at home. Now that I can find good, fresh tubs of crab meat at the supermarket I can really rely on this as a table-and-tummy filler when I don't have much time for slow, store-by-specialist-store shopping.

The quantities below provide generous amounts for four people, so this is the sort of starter that you can use to save you coming up with enormous amounts later on in the evening. I often halve it for a quick supper for the two of us at home, or when it's me and a girlfriend and a chilled bottle of rosé.

2 x 15 ml tablespoons mirin (Japanese sweet rice wine)
$^1/_2$ teaspoon wasabi paste
1 x 15ml tablespoon rice vinegar
few drops sesame oil
$^1/_2$ teaspoon Maldon salt or $^1/_4$ teaspoon table salt
1 long red chilli pepper, deseeded and finely chopped
200g crab meat
approx. 1 teaspoon lime juice
150g rocket salad
1 ripe avocado
1–2 teaspoons chopped chives

1 In a bowl that will take the crab meat later, whisk together the mirin, wasabi paste, rice vinegar, sesame oil and salt. Then remove about 4 teaspoons to another big bowl large enough to fit your salad.

2 To the first, more generous amount of dressing, add the finely chopped chilli and then the crab meat, and fork through to mix thoroughly.

3 To the small amount of dressing in the other bowl, add the lime juice and then the salad leaves and toss well to mix, before arranging on four plates.

4 Spoon a quarter of the mixture into a metal American $^1/_3$-cup measure, or a small ramekin, squishing down to get it all in, then unmould in the centre of a salad-lined plate. Just turn over, tap and the crab meat should fall out. Repeat with the remaining crab meat and the 3 other plates.

5 Using a rounded teaspoon measure, scoop out curls or humps of avocado and dot around on top of the salady bits. Spritz with a little lime juice.

6 Sprinkle the chopped chives over the mounds of crab and take the plates to the table.

Serves 4 as a starter

SAKÉ SEA BASS AND WILTED GREENS

WORKDAY WINNERS

This is very calm, very plain, very good. It's what I make for people on diets or who don't like anything too vigorous or when I feel in need of a Zen moment. I am aware that doesn't make it sound very exciting, but fresh fish really doesn't need anything to make it appetizing, it just needs to be allowed to be tasted. And this is the sort of elegant, pared-down food that's hard to get in a restaurant. If you want to have potatoes with it, then steam some, although this will take longer than the fish, but requires almost no effort.

Easier, though, to provide a little something first and make everyone happy with the confident restraint of just fabulous fish and some flavoursome wilted greens.

2 sea bass, approx. 900g each, gutted and prepared
4 spring onions
6 x 15ml tablespoons saké
2 x 15ml tablespoons soy sauce
1 teaspoon grated ginger

1 Preheat the oven to 200°C/gas mark 6. Lay each sea bass on a large piece of foil, and bring up the sides ready to make a parcel.

2 Slice the spring onions in half lengthways and place 4 pieces into the cavity of each fish.

3 Into each parcel, sprinkle 3 tablespoons of saké, 1 tablespoon of soy sauce, and about $^1/_2$ teaspoon of the grated ginger.

4 Wrap the parcels loosely but seal them firmly, and cook on a baking sheet in the oven for about 25 minutes.

5 Open the cooked fish parcels, peel away the skin from the top of each fish and fillet the top layer of fish.

6 Turn the fish over, and repeat the same process again, and then spoon over any juices from the parcel onto the filleted sea bass and serve with the wilted greens.

Serves 4–6

I use anything to hand: pak choi torn up small, mangetouts, spinach, assorted bits from the bottom of the vegetable drawer and salad compartment. This is the best way I've found of using up bags and bits of designer leaves that are past their best – not bad, but no longer beautiful enough to be served as salad.

2 x 15ml tablespoons garlic oil
2 anchovy fillets
approx. 500g assorted green vegetables

1 Heat the oil and anchovies in a wok or large, heavy-based pan and stir until the anchovies seem to start melting into the oil.

2 Toss in your green vegetables and stir-fry over a fairly high heat – a few minutes at the most – until everything has wilted.

Serves 4

BRANDIED-BACONY CHICKEN

I've never made a secret of my love and respect for a plain, old-fashioned, unreconstructed roast chicken. Why would I? But sometimes it's good to play, and the brandy and bacon here bring flavour (and help the bird bronze up beautifully) though not distraction. It's still what it is.

Alongside, I serve the Potato and Mushroom Gratin that follows and a lemony, crunchy green salad, *et c'est tout*. And if you want to dispense with the potato element altogether, I suggest this almost effort-free substitution: simply drain two cans of puy lentils, and when the chicken is roasted, and standing on a carving tray, warm up the lentils in the hot chickeny juices in the tin and serve as they are, sprinkled with parsley if you feel so inclined.

This is not speedy-speedy in actual cooking time but it's fantastically helpful when you have people for supper since all it requires is about 10 minutes' preparation, and then you can lay the table, have a drink, put on lipstick while everything cooks happily by itself in a hot oven.

2 rashers streaky bacon	6oml brandy
1 chicken, approx. 1.25kg	

1 Preheat the oven to 220°C/gas mark 7.

2 In a small frying pan, cook the bacon over a medium heat until it's crisp and the pan is full of lovely bacony fat, about 4 minutes.

3 Take the pan off the heat, then remove the bacon and put it straight into the cavity of the chicken, sitting the chicken breast-side up, in a roasting tin as you do so.

4 Pour the brandy into the still hot frying pan and let it bubble for a minute with the bacon fat.

5 Pour the brandy mixture over the chicken, place in the hot oven and roast for 45 minutes, or until the juices run clear between the leg and body. Let it rest for 10 minutes before carving.

Serves 4

POTATO AND MUSHROOM GRATIN

There are few sights in the kitchen as uplifting as a golden, bubbling gratin coming out of the oven, and this is the perfect accompaniment to the chicken, so everyone's happy. It's strange to be saying it, but one of the reasons I love this particular gratin is that it isn't too creamy and rich. And the relative thinness of the wine and milk that the potatoes and mushrooms are cooked in – relative to double cream, that is – is what allows you to cook this in such a hot oven and so quickly.

The first two times I cooked this, I peeled the potatoes; now I don't bother. It isn't necessary (and I buy baking potatoes which come all clean and shiny) and even if peeling them doesn't really take long, it's a good psychological step to remove: this is now a quick slice and chop, in a pan and then into the oven. It feels easy – but then that's because it is easy.

3 average-sized baking potatoes (approx. 750g total), thinly sliced	2 x 15ml tablespoons butter
	2 teaspoons garlic oil
	250g chestnut mushrooms, finely sliced
350ml full-fat milk	
3 x 15ml tablespoons white wine	salt and pepper to taste

1 Preheat the oven to 220°C/gas mark 7 and butter a shallow baking dish or gratin.

2 Bring the sliced potatoes, milk and white wine to boil in a saucepan, seasoning with salt and pepper to taste and stirring occasionally, then leave at a simmer while you get on with the mushrooms.

3 Warm the butter and oil in a frying pan over a medium-high heat. Add the mushrooms and cook, stirring occasionally, until softened, about 3 minutes.

4 Pour the mushrooms and their garlicky, buttery juices into the pan of potatoes, stir to mix and pour straight into the gratin dish. Bake in the oven, alongside the chicken, for 45 minutes, or until piping hot and crisp on top.

Serves 4

STEAK SLICE WITH LEMON AND THYME

This recipe, or rather the method, was suggested to me by my agent Ed Victor, and so is known familiarly as Ed's Tender Rump. The method is this: instead of marinating the meat before cooking, you marinate it *after*; it really does keep it extraordinarily tender. Please feel free to play around with the herbs; I think Ed himself uses oregano rather than the thyme I love.

I like this with *broccoletti* or those leggy tender-stem broccoli. A couple of packets, lightly cooked, drained, and sitting in the marinade after the beef's out and sliced, is the most heavenly accompaniment. And I can't tell you how good both steak and broccoli are cold later.

1 x 2.5cm-thick rump steak, approx. 600g	80ml extra virgin olive oil
5 stalks thyme, to give 1 x 15ml tablespoon stripped leaves	zest and juice of $1/2$ lemon
2 bruised cloves garlic	1 teaspoon Maldon salt or $1/2$ teaspoon table salt
	good grinding of fresh pepper

1 Cut away the fat from around the edge of the steak while you heat a griddle or heavy-based pan.

2 Brush the steak with oil to prevent it sticking to the griddle or pan, and cook for 3 minutes a side plus 1 minute each side turned again (this gives you pretty griddle marks) for desirably rare meat; the lemon in the post-hoc marinade "cooks" it a little more.

3 While the steak is cooking, place the thyme leaves, garlic, oil, lemon zest and juice, and salt and pepper in a wide, shallow dish.

4 Once the steak is cooked, place it in the dish of marinade for 4 minutes a side, before removing it to a board and slicing thinly on the diagonal.

Serves 4

SEARED SALMON WITH SINGAPORE NOODLES

I know the list of ingredients is long, but a lot of this is stuff that will help you generally if it's part of your storecupboard-stash. If you don't want to go in for specialist shopping at all (I love it, and now can indulge myself online, too), then replace the tiny dried shrimp with about 100g of small frozen (though thaw them first) prawns. Sherry could be used instead of the Chinese cooking wine, though I should tell you that I get this very easily from my local supermarket.

2 teaspoons medium Madras curry powder
1/4 teaspoon table salt

1 teaspoon sugar
4 salmon fillets, approx. 200g each
1 x 15ml tablespoon garlic oil

1 Mix the curry powder, salt and sugar in a wide, shallow dish and dredge the salmon in this, turning the pieces all over in the rub.

2 Heat the oil in a heavy-based pan and cook the salmon fillets on a high heat for about 2–3 minutes a side, searing the sides of the fillets too if they are very thick.

Serves 4

SINGAPORE NOODLES

250g vermicelli rice noodles
50g dried shrimp
125ml Chinese cooking wine
1 x 15ml tablespoon garlic oil
100g finely sliced Chinese leaf
125g baby corn, sliced into thin rounds
2 spring onions, finely sliced
2 teaspoons medium Madras curry powder

1 teaspoon finely chopped ginger
250ml chicken stock (from concentrate)
3 x 15ml tablespoons soy sauce
150g beansprouts
4 x 15ml tablespoons chopped fresh coriander

1 Put the rice noodles into a bowl and cover with boiling water. Leave them to soak for 4 minutes and then drain them.

2 Soak the dried shrimp in the wine, then heat the oil in a wok and fry the Chinese leaf, baby corn and spring onions for a few minutes.

3 Add the curry powder and finely chopped ginger to the wok, and then the chicken stock and soy sauce. Pour in the shrimps, with their wine, and the drained, soaked noodles, tossing and shaking everything all together in the wok.

4 Finally, stir in the beansprouts and give a final toss, before turning out into a bowl and sprinkling with the coriander.

LAYERED SALAD WITH ROAST QUAIL

WORKDAY WINNERS

This started off life in my kitchen as a layered salad with cold chicken in the mix, but I felt that the juicy crunchiness of the salad, and its glorious, bright simplicity didn't need to be fleshed out. Roast quail seemed to me to be in just the right register and, what's more, ridiculously easy to deal with. If you want, you can cook them a little ahead, since they're good warm rather than hot. And if there is salad and quail left over, then take the meat off the little birds and toss it in the salad the next day. Serve with a pile of (preferably warm) flat breads and quite a few finger bowls.

1 teaspoon Maldon salt or
$^1/_2$ teaspoon table salt
juice of 1 lemon
$^1/_2$ teaspoon dried mint (dried thyme
  is also good)
2 teaspoons honey
80ml olive oil
12 quail
250g cos (or romaine) lettuce, sliced
  into 1cm shreds

1 bunch (150g) radishes, trimmed and
  sliced into fine rounds
$^1/_2$ cucumber, part peeled to give a
  stripy effect and cut into 1cm
  chunks
1 red bell pepper, deseeded and cut
  into 1cm chunks
seeds from $^1/_2$ pomegranate
2 x 15ml tablespoons chopped mint
  leaves

1 Preheat the oven to 220°C/gas mark 7. Put the salt and lemon juice into a jar, add the dried mint, the honey and olive oil, then put on the lid and shake like mad.

2 Arrange the quail in a couple of small baking tins or foil trays, and pour half the jar of dressing over them, basting the baby birds well before they go in the oven.

3 Roast the quail for 30 minutes and, while they're cooking, get on with the salad.

4 Layer the salad ideally into a glass straight-sided bowl, drizzling a little of the remaining dressing on each layer, as follows: cos lettuce, radish slices, cucumber chunks, red pepper, more cos lettuce and then pomegranate seeds, with the chopped mint leaves sprinkled on top.

Serves 6–8

ETON MESS

There is no variation of this pudding I don't like, and I must have made several in my time. This one uses bottled fresh pomegranate juice to encourage the strawberries to ooze out their fragrant summery juices. If you're making this with out-of-season strawberries, then you stand a chance of using freshly squeezed pomegranate juice, in which case, sprinkle some seeds on top of this voluptuous mound of meringue and berry-spiked cream. (Any leftover meringues, could be sandwiched with ice cream, wrapped in clingfilm and stashed in the freezer to be eaten as snatched indulgences when the mood hits. Meringues never need to be thawed as they don't really freeze even in the freezer.)

500g strawberries
2 teaspoons caster or vanilla sugar
2 teaspoons pomegranate juice

500ml whipping cream
4 x small meringue nests from a packet

1 Hull and chop the strawberries and put into a bowl. Add the sugar and pomegranate juice and leave to macerate while you whip the cream.

2 Whip the cream in a large bowl until thick but still soft.

3 Roughly crumble in 4 meringues nests – you will need chunks for texture, as well as a little fine dust.

4 Take out a ladleful, or about 100g, of the chopped strawberries, and fold the meringued cream and rest of the fruit mixture together.

5 Arrange on four serving plates or glasses, or in a mound, and top each one with some of the remaining macerated strawberries.

Serves 4

CARIBBEAN CREAMS

This is a reworking of my grandmother's Barbados creams: we're going the way of the coconut and the banana. It's scarcely a fancy pudding, but sometimes it can be sweetly comforting to have something a little homespun, and almost from the nursery. This is not far from that old favourite, bananas mashed with cream and brown sugar. Hard to beat, to be sure, but the coconut yogurt and rum certainly add a little something.

You need to make these the morning of the evening you want to eat them (or the day before, if that's easier for you), but they take no more than 5 minutes to prepare. So they are very quick to make and you ease the burden on that short time after you get back from work in the evening.

WORKDAY WINNERS

175g coconut yogurt
175ml double cream
1 x 15ml tablespoon coconut rum, such as Malibu (optional)

1 banana
2 x 15ml tablespoons dark muscovado sugar

1 Stir together the yogurt and cream with the Malibu, if you're using it, and whisk until slightly thickened.

2 Slice the banana and then divide the slices between four 125ml-ramekins to form a layer at the bottom of each one.

3 Spoon in the thickened yogurt and cream mixture, filling the ramekins equally.

4 Sprinkle about 1$\frac{1}{2}$ teaspoons of sugar over each ramekin, then wrap them in clingfilm, and place in the fridge overnight or for the day.

Serves 4

FLOURLESS CHOCOLATE BROWNIES

However much people have eaten, there is always, I've noticed, room for a brownie. This is a different kind of a brownie, most definitely for party-pudding, melting, fudgy and damply rich. I compound these qualities by serving it with ice cream and the Hot Chocolate Sauce that follows, but there is no need. Need is not really what we're talking about here, though, is it?

225g dark chocolate, 70% cocoa solids
225g butter
2 teaspoons vanilla extract
200g caster sugar

3 eggs, beaten
150g ground almonds
100g chopped walnuts

1 Preheat the oven to 170°C/gas mark 3. Melt the chocolate and butter gently over a low heat in a heavy-based saucepan.

2 Take the pan off the heat, mix in the vanilla and sugar, and let it cool a little.

3 Beat the eggs into the pan along with the ground almonds and chopped walnuts. Turn into a 24cm square baking tin or, most sensibly, use a foil one.

4 Bake in the oven for 25–30 minutes, by which time the top will have set but the mixture will still be gooey. Once cooler, cut carefully, four down, four across, into 16 squidgy-bellied squares.

Makes 16 squares

HOT CHOCOLATE SAUCE

75g dark chocolate, 70% cocoa solids
125ml double cream
2 x 15ml tablespoons Camp coffee or 2 teaspoons instant espresso powder
    dissolved in 2 tablespoons water
1 x 15ml tablespoon golden syrup

1 Break up the chocolate and put into a heavy-based saucepan.

2 Add the remaining ingredients, then place the pan over a gentle heat and let everything melt together.

3 Once everything has melted, stir well, take off the heat and pour into a jug to serve.

Makes enough to drizzle over 16 brownie squares

BLACKBERRY CRISP

Another glorious nursery-reworking, and none the worse for that. I feel, in the interests of fair trading, I should probably name this Blackberry Soggy, since what is so more-ish about it is its butter-fudgy topping. But since "crisp" is what these kinds of non-crumble pies are known as, I'll stick to that.

It's simplicity itself to make, and the daughter of a friend of mine, who had never, ever made a pudding or baked anything before, has had a runaway success with it, that threatens to go, delightfully, to her head. A pudding this good quite reasonably causes evangelical fervour. Its ease of assembly is a bonus.

To keep the costs down, you could substitute half the blackberries with chopped pears, but, anyway, regard this as an open blueprint and use any fruit you feel like or that is to hand.

125g butter	1 teaspoon ground cinnamon
60g jumbo porridge oats	75g soft light brown sugar
40g flaked almonds	500g (4 punnets) blackberries
30g sunflower seeds	2 teaspoons cornflour
70g flour	50g vanilla sugar or caster sugar

1 Preheat the oven to 200°C/gas mark 6. Melt the butter in a small saucepan (or in a bowl in the microwave) and put to one side for a moment.

2 Combine the porridge oats, flaked almonds, sunflower seeds, flour, ground cinnamon and brown sugar in a bowl.

3 Tip the blackberries into a wide, shallow baking dish (I used one with a 750ml capacity). Sprinkle the cornflour and vanilla sugar over the berries, and tumble them about to mix.

4 Stir the melted butter into the crisp topping – that's the oat mixture – and spoon on top of the blackberries to partially, but not absolutely, cover them.

5 Bake in the oven for 25 minutes and serve with ice cream or thick cream.

Serves 4–6

CHOCOLATE MINT COOKIES

This is my version of after dinner mints: dispense with *dessert* and bring out a plate of minty breathed chocolate cookies with coffee and *tisanes* instead.

These don't take long to make up and bake, and I can't tell you how lovely it is to be able to open the door to people with the smell of their baking oozing welcomingly out in the evening air.

100g soft butter
150g light brown sugar
1 teaspoon vanilla extract
1 egg
150g flour
35g cocoa powder
$1/2$ teaspoon baking powder
200g dark chocolate chips

FOR THE GLAZE
75g icing sugar
1 x 15ml tablespoon cocoa, sieved
2 x 15ml tablespoons boiling water
$1/4$ teaspoon peppermint extract
(I use Boyajian Natural
Peppermint Flavour)

1 Preheat the oven to 180°C/gas mark 4.

2 Cream the butter and brown sugar (I use a freestanding mixer for ease), then beat in the vanilla extract and the egg.

3 Mix the flour, cocoa and baking powder in a bowl and gradually beat in to the creamed mixture. Finally, fold in the chocolate chips.

4 Using a rounded 15ml-tablespoon measure, spoon out scoops of cookie dough and place on a lined baking sheet, leaving a little space in between each one.

5 Bake in the oven for 12 minutes and then let them sit on the baking sheet for a couple of minutes before moving them to a cooling rack, with some newspaper on the surface underneath to catch any escaping glaze later.

6 Put the glaze ingredients into a saucepan and heat until combined.

7 Using a teaspoon, zig-zag the glaze over each cooling cookie.

Makes 26

Escoffier famously said that *la nostalgie*, or homesickness, was simply a longing for the food of one's childhood. As a Frenchman living in London at the turn of the twentieth century, he had reason to be mournful perhaps, but those of us who live in today's food-fashion obsessed Anglo world have cause for wistfulness, even if we haven't transplanted ourselves. So much of what we ate when young, or what our parents and grandparents ate when they were young, has disappeared.

I am not sure quite whether we shun the food of our past as irrelevant and outmoded because we are less rooted in our culinary traditions than the Continental Europeans, or because, having absorbed a sense of our gastro-inferiority and desperate to show our new coolth, we are too much afflicted with gawky irony. I suspect both conditions are linked. It is frankly inconceivable that anyone in France would feel that celeriac remoulade were embarrassingly antique or that an Italian might disdain spaghetti alla carbonara for being old-fashioned. The French and the Italians love their food precisely because it's old-fashioned – it is the food their grandparents ate – and they know their grandchildren will love it, too.

In other words, there is really no such thing, to the cook or to the eater, as retro. And yet here I am, lamenting our own shortcomings while almost seeming to relish that I possess them by virtue – or vice? – of this very chapter. So be it. There are too many reasons for our being as we are, to be able to disentangle or disinter now. Besides, I know what I mean by retro, and I know you do, too

Just as I think it's possible to feel an inherited nostalgia for the music one's parents listened to, so I concur that many of the recipes here more properly belong to the era of an earlier generation than mine. I love the idea – and am mad about the taste – of Crêpes Suzette and Pineapple Upside-Down Cake (see pages 75 and 82), for example, but I was scarcely brought up on them. Even worse, I feel myself becoming nostalgic for a period of nostalgia. All the cocktails, I drank in the eighties, were themselves a throwback, and self-consciously so: it was art deco only without the elegance. Yes, I did possess some black martini glasses – and yes, I have bought some recently, all the better to fill with White Lady (one part lemon juice to two parts Cointreau and four parts gin) and if that sounds like a camp folly, I should declare that it only looks like a joke.

And I suppose that's the thing: the affectation of amusement, the attitude of whimsical irony, they are just surface silliness. The real thing is that the food we remember, or remember our parents recalling with pleasure, is food we want to eat. There isn't one recipe that follows here which I don't relish purely for the way it tastes. For what I lack in sentimentality, I more than make up for in greed.

AVOCADO CRAYFISH COCKTAIL

I eat an enormous amount of avocados. Some people are repelled by their soft-clay richness; I am drawn to it. I remember, too, when I was really quite young, just into my teens, reading that the dogs which lived on avocado orchards always had shiny, glossy coats because of all the windfall fruit they snaffled up daily. That image has stuck with me, and it is such an appealing one. I always have it in mind as I prepare myself an avocado, which is often.

And when, the other day, I found myself buying a pair of old-fashioned avocado dishes, I knew I had to be a little more backward-looking in my style of eating (most often, I just sprinkle with Maldon salt and spritz with lime), so this is my version of the avocado prawn cocktail of yore. For me, it's the way forward.

1 tomato
½ teaspoon Maldon salt or
      ¼ teaspoon table salt
2 teaspoons sherry vinegar

1 teaspoon extra virgin olive oil
75g cooked peeled crayfish tails
1 ripe avocado
1 teaspoon chopped fresh coriander

1 Halve the tomato, scoop out and discard the seeds, and chop well what's left, dropping the pieces into a bowl with the salt, sherry vinegar and olive oil. Whisk to make a dressing.

2 Just before you want to eat, stir the crayfish tails into the dressing.

3 Halve the avocado, remove the stone and spoon the crayfish-tomato mixture into the hollows where the stone went, sprinkle with the coriander and serve at once.

Serves 2

SMOKED TROUT PÂTÉ

Smoked fish was an absolute staple of my childhood – I used to have smoked mackerel with horseradish in my lunchbox – and if I have some form of smoked fish in the fridge, I feel there is always going to be, instantly, something to eat. Pepper and lemon, that's all you need to add to it. And it's a gift to the cook in a hurry: this pâté takes the merest moment to make and yet it is a wonderful start to a meal or, indeed, a whole meal in itself. I don't even need a salad with it: I'm happy with toast, crusty bread, or maybe even some good shop-bought English muffins or cheese scones, along with a few cornichons (baby gherkins) and any other tangy pickle.

This doesn't make very much, but it's filling and also – which is obviously how I like it – full of pep. If you want something a little milder, with less boisterous heat, then add a mere sprinkling of cayenne.

2 smoked trout fillets, approx. 125g total weight

50g Philadelphia cream cheese

1 x 15ml tablespoon horseradish sauce

2 x 15ml tablespoons lemon juice

$^1/_4$ teaspoon cayenne pepper

2 x 15ml tablespoons olive oil

1 Put all the ingredients into a blender or food processor and blitz until smooth and pâté-like.

2 Spoon the mixture into a bowl (I use a small terracotta dish of about 12cm diameter), scraping out any mixture remaining in the processor with a spatula. Cover the bowl with clingfilm, and place in the fridge to chill.

Serves 4 as a starter

CHEF'S SALAD

I am no chef, so perhaps this should more correctly be called Cook's Salad. Either way, it is an irresistible mix, and one that tastes so much better in the mouth than it reads on the page.

I am unapologetic about celebrating the much-maligned iceberg, and feel perfectly equable about your using the ready-torn bits of lettuce in bags. I should own up that I keep a packet of ready-grated Emmental in the fridge, which I generally use in this. And there is something about canned sweetcorn that is instantly comforting, especially with the cool, soft chunks of avocado. It is, indeed, the glorious mix of textures that makes this salad such a knockout. How could it ever have fallen from favour?

1 head iceberg lettuce
225g ham, cut into 1cm cubes
1 x 195g can sweetcorn, to give 150g
    drained weight
75g grated Emmental
1 ripe avocado, peeled, stoned and cut
    into chunks

FOR THE DRESSING
$^1/_2$ teaspoon Dijon mustard
1 x 15ml tablespoon Cabernet
    Sauvignon vinegar
$^1/_2$ teaspoon Maldon salt or
    $^1/_4$ teaspoon table salt
3 x 15ml tablespoons extra virgin
    olive oil

1 Tear the iceberg lettuce into pieces into a large bowl.

2 Toss in the ham, drained sweetcorn, grated Emmental and avocado chunks.

3 Whisk together the dressing ingredients in a separate bowl, and then pour over the salad before tossing everything together.

Serves 6 as a starter; or 2–4 as a supper or lunch dish

Oeufs en Cocotte

My mother used to bake eggs for Sunday supper, most weeks, when I was a child – and I haven't eaten them since. Or at least not until recently, when I felt an urgent and greedy need to resurrect them. My mother used to cook them in a pretty low oven for 19 minutes, and 19 minutes exactly; since this is "express", I bake mine in a moderate oven for a quarter of an hour – and lusciously perfect they are, too.

The only other change I have made is an extravagant addition; I add a drop or two of white truffle oil over the cream, on top of the egg. Other flavour additions – a little chopped ham, diced cooked mushrooms, a few herbs, some sliced artichoke heart – should go on the base, before you crack in the egg.

This is a very comforting and yet luxurious starter, which is helpful in that you could give people this, followed by some plain chicken and a green salad, and they would consider they had feasted like oligarchs.

I am happy to spoon the creamy egg straight out of its ramekin dish, but some thick slabs of toasted sourdough or good wheaten bread, sliced into chunky fingers, are de rigueur as a tableside accompaniment. If you feel like pushing the boat out, throw in steamed asparagus spears, too.

butter for greasing
6 organic eggs
$1^1/_2$ x 15ml tablespoons Maldon salt

6 x 15ml tablespoons double cream
$1^1/_2$ x 15ml tablespoons white truffle oil

1 Preheat the oven to 190°C/gas mark 5, and put a full kettle of water on to boil.

2 Dip a pastry brush in some softened butter and grease six ramekins, each about 125ml capacity, putting them into an ovenproof tin or dish as you go.

3 If you're adding extras, put them into the ramekins now.

4 Crack an egg into each ramekin, followed by $^1/_4$ teaspoon of salt, 1 tablespoon of cream and, finally, $^1/_4$ teaspoon of the white truffle oil.

5 Pour boiling water into the tin or dish to come about halfway up each ramekin. Place in the oven and bake for 15 minutes. Serve immediately.

Serves 6

MOUCLADE

For some reason, this lesser-known cousin of moules marinière has gone out of fashion. That's to say, I haven't seen it on a menu or eaten it anywhere outside of my kitchen for yonks. And yet it's so good, with its creamy, mildly curried sauce.

This is very much a quick version: I use ready-washed, debearded mussels, then leeks or spring onions in place of chopped onion or shallot; and I don't sift, strain, reduce or anything like that. It means that this is slightly soupier than the traditional version, but all the better for that. Buy a baguette or two to mop up the fragrant, creamy juices and consider yourself among the truly blessed.

2kg mussels
4 baby leeks (or spring onions), finely sliced
2 cloves garlic, peeled and finely sliced
500ml white wine (or 250ml Noilly Prat and 250ml water)

2 teaspoons medium Madras curry powder
125ml double cream

1 Soak the mussels in some clean, cold water and – if they haven't been dealt with in the shop – sort through them, debearding, and knocking off any barnacles with the back of a small knife.

2 Take a large pan with a lid. Add the sliced baby leeks (or spring onions), sliced garlic, white wine (or Noilly Prat and water) and curry powder, and bring to the boil.

3 Tip the mussels into a colander, discarding any that haven't closed, and tumble the rest into the pan, clamp on the lid and cook on a high heat for about 3 minutes. Shake the pan around as they are cooking.

4 When you lift the lid, the mussels should have opened. Discard any that haven't. Add the double cream, and then turn into a bowl to serve, or take the pan straight to the table. Remember to put out plates for the shells.

Serves 4

CHICKEN LIVER SALAD

Now this is a real blast from the past for me. I started moonlighting as a restaurant critic during the great Gastronomic Renaissance, as everyone seemed to herald it, about 20 years ago, when I was an eager young thing, or almost, and there was scarcely a restaurant that didn't have a *salade tiède* of this sort on its menu. Generally, the dressing was made with raspberry vinegar, which was entirely the vogue, and I have tried to pay *hommage* to this in an echo of the sour-sweetness by deglazing the pan of chicken livers with sherry vinegar and maple syrup. OK, I know it sounds odd – rebarbative even – but it is a gorgeous pairing: only fugitively sweet but intense and smoky.

It also happens to be a very quick supper for two, and not the sort of quickly got-together meal that feels drearily samey.

2 x 15ml tablespoons olive oil
300g chicken livers
1 x 130g packet rocket salad
1 x 15ml tablespoon sherry vinegar

1 x 15ml tablespoon maple syrup
1 teaspoon Maldon salt or
   ¹/₂ teaspoon table salt

1 Heat the oil in a heavy-based frying pan and cook the livers for about 7 minutes, turning the livers about in the pan regularly and squishing them as you do so to help them cook evenly.

2 While they are cooking, arrange the salad on two plates.

3 Once the livers are cooked, their rawness inside turned to moussy pink, take the pan off the heat and quickly add the sherry vinegar and maple syrup.

4 Stir everything about, deglazing the pan, then divide the dressed livers between the two plates of salad and pour the juice from the pan over them.

5 Sprinkle with the salt and serve warm.

Serves 2

CHEESE FONDUE

I don't suppose this is ever going to win plaudits from the World Health Organization, but a cheese fondue is surely the stuff of dreams. On the plus side, health-wise, I love it best with radishes, chicory, spears of radicchio and carrots dipped in, but I don't know why I am trying to engage with that particular argument. The point is, it makes a fabulous supper: filling, gorgeous to eat and conducive to a good atmosphere and even better spirits.

Make a vat of this, and supply nothing other than fruit afterwards or, at most, a little palate-tickling sorbet.

600g chopped or grated cheese (use a mixture such as Gruyère, Emmental, Brie and Camembert)
300ml white wine
2 teaspoons cornflour
3 x 15ml tablespoons Kirsch
1 clove garlic, peeled
good grinding of pepper
good grating of nutmeg

TO SERVE
carrot batons, trimmed radishes, radicchio and chicory cut into spears or skinny wedges, cubes of toasted sourdough and whatever else you wish to dip

1 Put the chopped or grated cheese into the fondue pot with the wine and heat until boiling on the hob, by which time the cheese should have melted.

2 Turn the pot down to a simmer. Slake the cornflour with the Kirsch in a small bowl, and add to the fondue pot along with the garlic clove.

3 Season with the pepper and nutmeg, stir well and place the fondue pot over a flame at the table.

Serves 4

GOUJONS OF SOLE WITH DILL MAYONNAISE

Goujons have fallen from grace, but it is hard to work out why. The crunch of the bread-crumb casing, the tender, yielding softness of the white fish within: this is a fish finger taken to the highest level. If you can find the Japanese seasoned breadcrumbs, panko, then get them: they create an almost feathery but crunchy casing. The traditional accompaniment is a sauce tartare, but my favourite sauce is a dill mayonnaise, with perhaps some cornichons heaped on a plate nearby.

Consider these a fabulously quick starter when you've got people over or a real treat of a midweek supper for two. The trick is to prepare ahead for that. I make up a vast batch of these and freeze them. Then, when it's dinnertime and I don't know what I'm going to cook, I heat some oil in a pan and fry a handful from frozen. They barely need an extra minute. I prefer to fry in batches in a small saucepan rather than fill a frying pan with lots of oil and try to get them all done at once.

2 lemon sole fillets, skinned	250ml groundnut or grapeseed oil, or
70g cornflour	as needed (depending on size of
100g breadcrumbs or panko	pan)
2 eggs	salt and pepper

1 Cut the sole fillets in half lengthways, and then slice each fillet half into about four long strips on the diagonal. This will give you eight goujons from each fillet.

2 Put the cornflour into a shallow bowl and season with salt and pepper. Put the bread-crumbs or panko into another shallow bowl, and beat the eggs in an additional bowl.

3 Dip each goujon into the seasoned cornflour, coating it well, then the beaten egg, and finally the breadcrumbs.

4 Lay the goujons on a cooling rack for a while, and heat the oil in a pan. (Or at this point you can freeze them in layers of baking parchment in an airtight container.)

5 Fry the goujons for about 2 minutes, or until crisp and golden. Remove to pieces of kitchen paper as you go, to get rid of excess oil.

Makes 16, enough for about 3 people as a main course; 5 as a starter

DILL MAYONNAISE

200g mayonnaise, preferably organic	$^1/_2$–1 teaspoon lime juice to taste
15g (small bunch) dill	salt and pepper to taste

1 Put the mayonnaise into a bowl, and finely chop the dill, adding it to the mayo.

2 Stir in some lime juice and taste for seasoning.

CRÊPES SUZETTE

This is probably the queen of retro desserts and deservedly so. My version is a speeded-up and simplified one by virtue of using shop-bought crêpes. But there is no need to feel this is a cop-out. For one, they can be incredibly good but, more pertinently, by the time they've been doused and soused, not to mention, flamed, the idea that you could discern their origins is laughable.

If you have only ever thought of crêpes Suzette as some amusing vestige from an irrelevant culinary canon, think again. No, just forget that thought and cut straight to the cooking.

RETRO RAPIDO

juice of 2 oranges
zest of 1 orange
175g butter
75g caster sugar

8–12 shop-bought crêpes
80ml Grand Marnier, Cointreau or
    Triple sec

1 Pour the orange juice into a saucepan, and add the zest, butter and sugar. Bring to the boil, and then turn the heat down to a simmer, cooking for a further 10–15 minutes, until the sauce becomes syrupy.

2 Fold the crêpes into quarters and then arrange them in a large pan, or any flameproof dish, in a circular pattern and slightly overlapping each other.

3 Pour the warm syrup over the crêpes and then gently warm them through for about 3 minutes over a low heat.

4 Warm the orange liqueur of your choice in the emptied but still syrupy saucepan. When the crêpes are hot in the orange sauce, pour the liqueur over them and set light to the pan to flambé them. Serve immediately, spooning crêpes and sauce onto each plate.

Serves 4–6

MANGO SPLIT

Even when I was young, a banana split had begun to lose its glory, but the notion – fruit combined with ice cream and sauce – is a good one. I take advantage of what the Covent Garden traders used to refer to as "queer gear", and replace the world's favourite, because it's the least fruity, fruit with cubed mango. Rather lazily, I often buy the mangoes that my greengrocer, and all supermarkets, chop for you.

Incidentally, this is one of my children's favourite puddings, though I leave out the rum and coconut for them. For me, both resolutely stay in. I am of the More is More school in this regard.

2 x 15ml tablespoons shredded coconut
1 x 15ml tablespoon butter
50g soft light brown sugar
1 x 15ml tablespoon lime juice
1 x 15ml tablespoon dark rum
1 ball candied stem ginger (optional)

1 ripe mango or 1 tub ready-cubed
   ripe mango
2 scoops vanilla ice cream
2 scoops mango sorbet
2 cigar cookies or fan wafers (optional)

1 Toast the coconut in a dry smallish frying pan until dark golden and giving off a heady aroma. Transfer to a small bowl to cool.

2 In a saucepan, melt the butter, then combine with the sugar, lime juice and rum, let it come to a boil and bubble for 2 minutes. Turn off the heat but leave the pan on the hob.

3 Finely chop the candied ginger (if using) and peel then dice the mangoes (if not ready-cubed) into about 1cm cubes.

4 Place a scoop each of vanilla ice cream and mango sorbet onto two dessert bowls or into two sundae glasses.

5 Tumble the mango cubes, then the sticky-chopped ginger into each dish, and sprinkle the aromatically toasted coconut on top.

6 Spoon the still warm syrup over the fruit; there isn't a huge amount per dish but you don't want it swamped.

7 If the mood takes you, stick a cigar cookie or fan wafer into each sundae.

Serves 2

CHERRY CHEESECAKE

This recipe has overturned a lifetime's prejudice – which is good, but unsettling. I had always been a committed believer that the only true cheesecake was the proper, baked cheesecake, but now I'm not so sure. This improper, unbaked cheesecake, feature of many a seventies' dessert trolley, has entirely won me over. It's light, it has tang, and it is rapturously good. The fact that it is speedily easy to make is more reason for general hilarity and joy.

Even in the spirit of retro-accuracy, please do not be tempted to open a jar of cherry pie filling over the cake. I use some French cherry concoction that seems to be pretty universally available and has no added sugar, but anything labelled "conserve" as opposed to "jam" should be safe.

And, if you feel like it, when cherries are in season, strew the top with a couple of handfuls of beautiful fruit.

125g digestive biscuits
75g soft butter
300g cream cheese
60g icing sugar
1 teaspoon vanilla extract

$^1/_2$ teaspoon lemon juice
250ml double cream
1 x 284g jar St Dalfour Rhapsodie de
    Fruit Black Cherry Spread

1 Blitz the biscuits in a food processor until beginning to turn to crumbs, then add the butter and whiz again to make the mixture clump.

2 Press this mixture into a 20cm springform tin; press a little up the sides to form a slight ridge.

3 Beat together the cream cheese, icing sugar, vanilla extract and lemon juice in a bowl until smooth.

4 Lightly whip the double cream, and then fold it into the cream cheese mixture.

5 Spoon the cheesecake filling on top of the biscuit base and smooth with a spatula. Put it in the fridge for 3 hours or overnight.

6 When you are ready to serve the cheesecake, unmould it and spread the black cherry over the top.

Serves 6–8

PINEAPPLE UPSIDE-DOWN CAKE

This is a bit before my time, but I have vague nursery memories of a friend of my grand-mother's making a version of this, which she would serve with a warm sauce made of pineapple juice thickened with – I imagine – cornflour. That I can do without, but I am still of the mind that it is perfectly all right to make this with canned pineapple rings. I feel it is slightly bad sport to start peeling and slicing your own pineapple.

Anyway, canned pineapple is just fine, though I advise going for the one in its own juice rather than in syrup, and I add some of the juice to the sponge, too. This seems to help make it light and fluffy.

I have found that the best way of keeping this swift, is by baking it in my copper tarte Tatin tin; if you are using a regular cake tin, be prepared to add a few minutes on to the cooking time.

butter for greasing	100g flour
2 x 15ml tablespoons sugar	1 teaspoon baking powder
6 slices pineapple from a 425g can, plus 3 x 15ml tablespoons of the juice	$1/4$ teaspoon bicarbonate of soda
	100g soft butter
11 glacé cherries, approx. 75g total weight	100g caster sugar
	2 eggs

1 Preheat the oven to 200°C/gas mark 6. Butter a tarte Tatin tin (24cm wide at the top and 20cm diameter at the bottom) or use a 23cm cake tin (neither loose-bottomed nor springform).

2 Sprinkle the 2 tablespoons of sugar on top of the buttered base, and then arrange the pineapple slices to make a circular pattern as in the picture.

3 Fill each pineapple ring with a glacé cherry, and then dot one in each of the spaces in between.

4 Put the flour, baking powder, bicarbonate of soda, butter, caster sugar and eggs into a food processor and run the motor until the batter is smooth. Then pour in the 3 table-spoons of pineapple juice to thin it a little.

5 Pour this mixture carefully over the cherry-studded pineapple rings; it will only just cover it, so spread it out gently.

6 Bake for 30 minutes, then ease a spatula around the edge of the tin, place a plate on top and, with one deft – ha! – move, turn it upside-down.

Serves 8

don't wish to sound unsympathetic. Obviously, the fact that I am writing a book *expressly* concerned, as it were, with good food that can be got together quickly establishes, I hope, my bona fides in this regard. But I have to own up to some degree of impatience. The thing is, whenever people – perhaps showing a slightly patronizing amusement at how often I cook (and maybe it's this that irks) – claim that they never have the time to cook, it makes me feel uncharacteristically aggressive. What I want to point out is that they are hardly using the time they save by *not* cooking to write *War and Peace*. I don't suggest that finding time to cook makes you a better person, but nor do I think that being "too busy" to cook means that your life automatically has a higher purpose. And I say that as one who often professes to be beyond busy but somehow finds time to slump in front of the TV watching *CSI* repeats for hours on end.

The times when I do have ready sympathy with the too-frazzled-and-fraught-to-cook brigade is after children's birthday parties and at breakfast. I am not good at breakfast. I eat it because I know I must, but given a choice I would rather wait until later on in the day. Besides, since I must have two cups of tea before I even come to, it often leaves little time for fiddling around with breakfast, especially if your morning involves, as mine does, the taking of children to school.

The way of coping, I have found, is to be rather unimaginative about what you eat on waking. Just as I never got to work on time in the long-gone days when I had an office job, without laying out the morning's clothes before I went to bed at night, so I find I can speed through my tasks a little faster in the morning if I know in advance what I'm going to eat for breakfast. One moment's hesitation and I become a victim of choice, over-indulged and petulant and unable to be pleased.

What this means, in effect, is that I have month- or six-week-long tranches of any given breakfast – soft boiled egg with toast, porridge with blueberries, muesli with yogurt and pomegranate seeds, to cite recent examples – before sliding on to the next rotation. For weekdays, I think this makes perfect sense. But at weekends or when we're not at work, it can feel liberating to live beyond the routine.

I'm also happier to eat lunch later at weekends and therefore want a bigger breakfast, an hour or so after I've "tea'd" myself into consciousness. That's not to say all the recipes that follow couldn't be done during the week – they could, and easily. So please. Over to you.

Go Get 'Em Smoothie

This is truly a weekday special: a breakfast that combines food and drink for people who don't feel they've even got time to sit down in the morning.

If the person-in-a-hurry is miniature in stature, and has not progressed to caffeine intake, then replace the Camp coffee with a tablespoonful of peanut butter. Extra protein and ultra delicious.

I keep overripe bananas, peeled and cut into four, in bags in the freezer, which help give ice-creamy bulk to the smoothie and dispense with the need for ice.

1 peeled banana cut into 4, from the freezer
150ml milk of your choice
1 x 15ml tablespoon honey

4 teaspoons chocolate Ovaltine
1 teaspoon Camp coffee (or $^1/_2$ teaspoon instant espresso powder)

1 Put all the ingredients into a blender and whiz to mix.

2 Pour into a tall glass and drink before dashing out of the door.

Serves 1

CHOPPED FRUIT SALAD

This is my idea of an invigorating weekday breakfast, and I make an already easy recipe even more manageable by chopping up the fruit the evening before and leaving it in covered bowls in the fridge. I know that some people might worry about the lessening of vitamin content, but I assure you that unless you grow your own fruit or get up bright and early and buy it from a farmer who's just picked his, then you might as well not worry about how many vitamins you're losing by a little bit of in-advance chopping. Better to eat it pre-chopped than not at all, to be frank, and I also rather like the swallowing without chewing aspect that a little steeping gives.

What follows is the fruit I tend to use, although the key here is really to use what you already have in the fridge. The pomegranate juice below is out of a bottle, but if you're using out-of-season strawberries, add a squeeze of real juice to steep the berries and replace the mixed seeds with a gloriously jewelled topping of pomegranate seeds instead.

250g strawberries, finely chopped to make a cupful
1 teaspoon pomegranate juice
100g diced mango
½ teaspoon lime juice

125g blueberries
150g organic vanilla yogurt
2 teaspoons mixed seeds (pumpkin, sunflower, sesame)

1 Mix the chopped strawberries with the pomegranate juice.

2 Spritz the mango cubes with the lime juice.

3 Using two tumblers or glasses, layer the ingredients: strawberry, mango, blueberries, yogurt and, finally, the seeds.

Serves 2

BREAKFAST BRUSCHETTA

Something that is served, from California to Tuscany, as an evening savoury or appetizer may not seem an obvious choice for breakfast, but I say: think again. This is quick to make, absurdly easy in fact. The strange thing is that it is as easy to eat, even first thing. I can wolf this stuff down.

FOR THE TOMATO BRUSCHETTA
2 x 15ml tablespoons olive oil
2 thickly sliced short pieces
    sourdough or rustic toast
1 ripe tomato (approx. 100g), roughly
    chopped
salt and pepper to taste

FOR THE AVOCADO BRUSCHETTA
1 ripe avocado
2 teaspoons lime juice
4 thickly sliced short pieces
    sourdough or rustic toast
salt and pepper to taste
1 tablespoon chopped fresh parsley

1   To make the tomato bruschetta: drizzle most of the olive oil over each piece of toast and top with the chopped tomatoes. Season with salt and pepper to taste, before drizzling the remaining few drops of oil on top, and you're done.

2   To make the avocado bruschetta: halve the avocado; scoop the flesh into a bowl, along with the lime juice, then mash roughly, using a fork, and season to taste. Spread clumpingly on each waiting piece of toast and sprinkle with the parsley.

Serves 3–6, depending on appetite

HOME-MADE INSTANT PANCAKE MIX

This is going to change your life irrevocably. Forgive any scintilla of self-congratulatory preening and accept my boast as simple, enthusiastic exuberance. That is the spirit in which it is intended. But I tell you: just mix the ingredients below, keep them in a container at easy reach and then every time you are required to be the usher-forth of good things of a morning, you just scoop some dry mixture out, mix and whisk together with egg, milk and melted butter, by hand or in a blender – and that's it. Pancakes aplenty, without even having to think about it. You know it makes sense.

FOR THE PANCAKE MIX
600g flour
3 x 15ml tablespoons baking powder
2 teaspoons bicarbonate of soda

1 teaspoon salt
40g vanilla or caster sugar

1 Mix all the ingredients together and store in a jar.

2 When ready to make the pancakes, proceed as below.

TO MAKE THE BATTER AND THE PANCAKES
For each 150g pancake mix, add and whisk together:
1 egg
250ml semi-skimmed or full-fat milk
1 x 15ml tablespoon melted butter

1 Heat a flat griddle or pan with no oil.

2 Spoon drops of $1^1/_2$–2 tablespoons of batter onto the hot griddle or into the pan and, when bubbles appear on the surface of the little pancakes, flip them over to make them golden brown on both sides. A minute or so a side should do it.

Makes 15 pancakes, each about 8cm in diameter

BLUEBERRY SYRUP FOR PANCAKES

According to those who make it their business to know such things, both maple syrup and blueberries are supremely health-giving and wondrously good for you. This is fine by me, since I love them, separately and – by way of a new experiment – in combination. If you have any made-up syrup left over, you will notice that it sets into a kind of glossy jam. This will keep for a few days decanted into a jar and put in the fridge, and is glorious dolloped into yogurt or spread on bread.

125ml maple syrup
200g blueberries

1 Put the syrup and blueberries into a pan and bring to the boil.

2 Let bubble for 2–3 minutes, then pour into a jug and bring to the breakfast table with the pancakes.

Makes enough for the pancakes, above

BREAKFAST BARS

I am addicted to these, and so is everyone I give them to. Although they're quick to throw together, they do take nearly an hour to bake, so what I suggest is, make a batch at the weekend and then you will have the oaty, chewy bars ready and waiting for those days when you have to snatch breakfast on the hoof.

Mind you, they are just like milk and cereal in bar form, so there's nothing to stop you nibbling at one with your morning coffee at home every day. If you are not a morning person, believe me, they will make your life easier.

They also store well; indeed, they seem to get better and better. So just stash a tin with them and remove as and when you want.

1 x 397g can condensed milk	125g mixed seeds (pumpkin,
250g rolled oats (not instant)	sunflower, sesame)
75g shredded coconut	125g natural unsalted peanuts
100g dried cranberries	

1 Preheat the oven to 130°C/gas mark $^1/_2$, and oil a 23 x 33 x 4cm baking tin, or use a throw-away foil one.

2 Warm the condensed milk in a large pan.

3 Meanwhile, mix together all the other ingredients and then add the warmed condensed milk, using a rubber or wooden spatula to fold and distribute.

4 Spread the mixture into the tin and press down with the spatula or, better still, your hands (wearing disposable vinyl gloves to stop you sticking), to even the surface.

5 Bake for 1 hour, then remove from the oven and, after about 15 minutes, cut into four across, and four down to make 16 chunky bars. Let cool completely.

Makes 16

PEAR AND GINGER MUFFINS

These are particularly good: nothing fancy (I hate a breakfast muffin that thinks it's a cake), but the pear keeps the texture luscious and the ginger permeates everything, including your kitchen, with its husky heat. This makes for the kind of Saturday breakfast I can happily settle in to. And I'm pretty keen on a quick snack later on in the day of one of these now cooled muffins with some sharp, hard cheese, a Davidstow Cheddar maybe or Caerphilly, or a crumbly, pungent blue.

You can mix all the dry ingredients in a bowl, and the wet ones in a jug, cover both with clingfilm, and leave the former in a cool spot in the kitchen and the latter in the fridge. Then all you have to do is peel and chop the pear and fork everything lazily together in the morning. I dare say you will not get punished from on high if you don't bother to peel the pear, either. I do, simply because I love the way the juicy fruit merges with the crumb when there are no barriers to its oozing.

250g flour
2 teaspoons baking powder
150g caster sugar
75g light brown sugar, plus
$^1/_2$ teaspoon per muffin for
sprinkling
1 teaspoon ground ginger
1 x 142ml pot sour cream

125ml vegetable oil
1 x 15ml tablespoon honey
2 eggs
1 large pear such as a Comice (or
other fruit to give you about 300g
in weight), peeled, cored and cut
into 5mm dice

1 Preheat the oven to 200°C/gas mark 6, and line a 12-bun muffin tin with muffin papers.

2 Measure into a bowl the flour, baking powder, caster sugar, 75g of brown sugar and the ground ginger.

3 In a large measuring jug, whisk together the sour cream, oil, honey and eggs and then fold into the dry ingredients.

4 Lastly, mix in the diced pear, and divide the batter evenly between the muffin cases.

5 Sprinkle each one with $^1/_2$ teaspoon of brown sugar and bake for 20 minutes. Remove to a cooling rack. Best eaten still a little warm.

Makes 12

CHOCOLATE CROISSANTS

First, let me say that if I can do this, you can. As I have never tried to hide, I have no patience and even less dexterity. But this is child's play: indeed, you could consider getting children to make them. They certainly like eating them, and they tend to like eating what they make themselves even more.

1 x 375g packet ready-rolled butter puff pastry
1 x 100g dark chocolate bar (minimum 70% cocoa solids) or best-quality milk chocolate bar for children
1 egg, beaten

1   Preheat the oven to 220°C/gas mark 7. Unfurl the sheet of pastry and then cut it into six squares.

2   Cut each square diagonally to give 2 triangles (they will appear quite small). Put the triangle with the wider part facing you, and the point away from you.

3   Break off small pieces of chocolate (approx. 1cm) to place on the pastry triangles, about 2cm up from the wide end nearest you.

4   Then carefully roll from that chocolate-loaded end towards the point of the triangle.

5   You should now have something resembling a straight croissant. Seal it slightly with your fingertips and curl it around into a crescent.

6   Place the 12 chocolate croissants on a lined but not buttered baking tray and paint with the beaten egg. Bake for 15 minutes until they are golden and puffy and exuberantly, if miniaturely, croissant-like.

Makes 12

ORANGE FRENCH TOAST

There is not a type of French toast I don't love, but this version – a kind of eggy, squidgy toast and marmalade – is the perfect mixture between morning-sharp and weekend treatiness.

2 eggs
grated zest of 1 orange
60ml full-fat milk
$1/4$ teaspoon ground cinnamon
2 large, thick slices white bread or
    4 smaller slices

juice of 1 orange
75g fine-cut marmalade, such as
    Tiptree "crystal"
50g caster sugar
1 x 15ml tablespoon butter

1 Whisk the eggs, orange zest, milk and ground cinnamon in a wide shallow dish.

2 Soak the bread slices in this mixture for 2 minutes a side.

3 While the eggy bread is soaking, bring the orange juice, marmalade and sugar to the boil in a saucepan, then turn down the heat to a fast simmer for 3–4 minutes. If you need to, let this syrup stand while you cook the bread.

4 Heat the butter in a heavy-based frying pan and cook the eggy bread for about 2 minutes a side over a medium heat until golden.

5 Serve the French toast with some of the amber syrup poured over each slice, and a jug of extra syrup on the side.

Serves 2

GREEN EGGS AND HAM

This weekend breakfast favourite can, frankly, be eaten at any time of the day with equal relish and has also in its favour that children (who in my experience would probably eat anything if it had pesto in it) love it. This is entirely proper, of course, given that – very obviously – the recipe is inspired by the Good Doctor.

What you're making, in effect, is pesto pancakes – and these will be better if you use that "fresh" pesto that comes in a tub, not in a jar – which can be whizzed up in a blender and then needs a moment or two in a hot pan before being wrapped around finely sliced, tenderly pink ham.

75g pesto	150ml semi-skimmed milk
1 egg	oil for frying
75g flour	5 large thin slices of ham

1   Blend or whisk together the pesto, egg, flour and milk to make a batter.

2   Oil a crêpe pan or heavy-based frying pan, wiping away any excess oil with some kitchen paper, and place over a medium heat.

3   Ladle in approximately 100ml of batter, swirling instantly to gain a paper-thin crêpe.

4   Once the top becomes dry and the edges lift away, flick it over with a thin rubber or wooden spatula to cook the other side for about 30 seconds.

5   Layer the pancakes between pieces of baking parchment or greaseproof paper as you go, and when you have finished making them, lay a slice of ham on each one and roll up or fold into triangles – or however you like!

Makes 5

FRITTATA PARTY!

I love the sort of thin omelettes the Italians sometimes turn into sandwiches: cold and pressed between two pieces of mayonnaised bun or slices of *schiacciata* – an Italian flat-bread. And that's what I'd warmly advise here in the unlikely event that you end up with leftovers. But these are so good hot and straight off the press, eaten either with a knife and fork or rolled up within a warmed tortilla, that I urge you to morph into a kind of "short order omelette" cook next time you have a batch of people to feed convivially in the morning, or not long after.

The way to make this easy is, first get a good pan (I like a Scanpan Crêpe Pan), then get out loads of eggs and leave them out near a mixing bowl by the cooker, and then mix up a few ideas for fillings, setting them out ready in their bowls nearby. Then, all you do is crack two eggs, add your filling, fry, toss out and get on with the next.

I've jotted down what I put in the omelettes opposite. Obviously, I don't expect you to be restricted, but I thought it might be helpful.

FOR EACH OMELETTE
2 eggs
1/2 teaspoon butter and drop of oil
    for frying

FOR THE GREEN OMELETTE
20g watercress or baby spinach
    (or, indeed, rocket), finely chopped
1 spring onion, finely sliced

FOR THE CHEESE OMELETTE
25g grated Emmental (but any cheese
    should do)

FOR THE HAM OMELETTE
50g chopped ham

FOR THE CHILLI OMELETTE
1 long red chilli, deseeded and sliced
1/4 teaspoon ground ginger
1/4 teaspoon ground coriander

1 Beat the eggs with the filling of your choice.

2 Heat a crêpe pan or heavy-based frying pan with the butter and oil.

3 Once the pan is hot, pour in the egg mixture, swirling quickly to get an even and thin coating in the pan.

4 Let the omelette cook for a couple of minutes over a medium high heat.

5 Lift the edge of the omelette with a thin rubber spatula to check it is set and golden underneath; the top of the omelette should be just-about-set but still a little gooey.

6 Slip the omelette out of the pan onto a plate and flip one half of the omelette over the other, or fold in three like a business letter. Carry on!

GET UP AND GO

104

CROQUE MONSIEUR BAKE

Like many good brunch recipes, this is also just the ticket for an early evening supper, the sort you eat in your dressing gown before sophisticated adults feel it is entirely proper to dine.

The joy of this is that you make up the mustardy ham and Gruyère sandwiches and cover with beaten eggs the night before, and just let them sit in the fridge melding into one savoury, gooey pudding overnight. The next morning goes as follows: oven on; egg-and-bread dish in; brunch effortlessly served.

6 slices ready-sliced multigrain brown
   bread
75g Dijon mustard
125g (6 slices) of Gruyère slices
70g (3 slices) ham
6 eggs
1 teaspoon Maldon salt or
   $^1/_2$ teaspoon table salt

80ml full-fat milk
4 tablespoons grated Gruyère,
   Emmental or Cheddar
good sprinkling of Worcestershire
   sauce

1 Spread each slice of bread with mustard. Make sandwiches by putting each slice of cheese against the mustardy bread, and a slice of ham between them. Cut each sandwich in half to make two triangles.

2 Squish the sandwich triangles into an ovenproof dish approx. 27 x 21 x 6cm.

3 Beat together the eggs, salt and milk (I measure out the milk into whatever the mustard's been in for maximum flavour penetration) and then pour this over the sandwiches tightly packed in the dish.

4 Cover the dish with clingfilm and leave in the fridge overnight.

5 Next morning, preheat the oven to 200°C/gas mark 6. Take the dish out of the fridge and remove the clingfilm.

6 Sprinkle with the grated cheese and Worcestershire sauce and bake in the oven for 25 minutes.

Serves 4–6

have never quite understood why some people are obsessed with how long a recipe takes or, rather, how long something actually takes to cook. Certainly, I would never suggest you embark on my slow-cooked, 24-hour pork when you get home from work at seven and have people coming to eat at eight. That would be silly. But for most of our lives, the time it takes for something to cook is the least stressful aspect: what you should be considering is how much time *you* are required to spend in the kitchen. This is why, when I'm tired and lacking in impetus and inspiration, I would so much rather put a chicken in to roast – which will take an hour or so to cook, during which time I am not needed – than start chopping up things to stir-fry, which might take only 10 minutes but for all of those 10 minutes I will be required to busy myself frenetically.

I exult in the liberation that comes from slow-cooking. And I adore the feeling of security and messy organization that emanates from the cosy knowledge that there is something gently braising away in the oven or, even, still snugly wrapped in the fridge, ready and waiting for its oven time. This, for me, is one of the small pleasures of every-day life. It makes me feel involved in the kitchen, with food, when I'm busy elsewhere. I can't set aside huge tracts of time to get every meal ready when it's needed, so what I do is a little bit of prep here and there, a five-minute think-about-and-plan, so that when I do need to cook, it's nearly all taken care of. All I have to do is apply heat.

I don't have a vigorous do-it-ahead plan of attack, but I try to take some of the steps early. I stash steaks and chicken portions into marinades so that I've got something ready to be flung on a griddle without forethought at the end of the day. And the one thing I feel utterly beaten by when I'm really tired is the idea of peeling and chopping onions. I don't actually find it difficult, but the thought is a daunting one. So, when I have time to spare (usually when I'm avoiding something I should be doing), I peel, chop and fry onions slowly and gently to a gorgeous mush which can be frozen in cubes and then thawed to form the basis for a stew or sauce when needed.

I also like a small amount of quietly satisfying jar-filling in my life. It's scarcely strenuous, deeply enjoyable and also means you have the wherewithal for pudding when-ever you want at some unforeseen future point. I fill a jar with golden sultanas, pour Grand Marnier over them and let them steep. I've also been known to go the more traditional rum 'n' raisin route, and very good they both are. I put morello cherries and cherry brandy in a jar, and – a very recent innovation and rubily gorgeous – mix dried cherries and berries, that's how they're labelled, with a pomegranate liqueur called Pama. Any of these are exquisite tumbled over ice cream.

Slow-cooking, quite simply, can be the express route. When you think about it, there is almost a cosmic pathos about our contemporary belief that you can "save" time. I can save you energy and, importantly, stress.

Besides, I can't live every minute of my life as a spinning top, whipping myself to go ever faster. My quick-quick-slow approach isn't just about offering practical help; it actually changes the emotional tenor of the house, as you will find out.

Maple Chicken 'n' Ribs

This recipe says it all. You need no more than a few minutes to load up a couple of freezer bags with ribs and chicken, oils and unguents and then, after a day or so's untroublesome marinating in the fridge, you tip out the contents into a roasting tray and slot it in the oven. Your input is minimal, but what you get out is a big feast that feels homey and welcoming and makes everyone happy, you included.

12 pork spare ribs
12 chicken thighs, skin and bone still on
250ml apple juice, as sharp as possible
4 x 15ml tablespoons maple syrup

2 x 15ml tablespoons vegetable oil
2 x 15ml tablespoons soy sauce
2 star anise
1 cinnamon stick, halved
6 cloves garlic, unpeeled

1 Put the ribs and chicken pieces in a couple of large freezer bags or into a dish.

2 Add the remaining ingredients, squelching everything together well, before sealing the bag or covering the dish.

3 Leave to marinate in the fridge overnight or up to two days.

4 When the marinating time is up, take the dish out of the fridge and preheat the oven to 200°/gas mark 6.

5 Pour the contents of the freezer bag into one or two large roasting tins (making sure the chicken is skin-side up), place in the oven and cook for about an hour and a quarter, by which time everything should be sticky and glossed conker-brown.

Serves 6–8

CRISPY DUCK

I've always thought one of the best ways to eat duck was as the Chinese do, but I had never thought it would be so easy to cook. I say "cook". I do nothing except cut some fat off the duck and sit it on a rack on a roasting tin and put it in the oven for hours on end. Then, I take it out, set to with some forks and put some shop-bought Chinese pancakes on to steam. I chop and slice cucumber and spring onions and open a jar of Hoisin sauce. Actually, come to think of it, I nearly always ask someone else to open it for me. This just could hardly be easier. What's more, children seem to adore it, which makes it a really lovely family Saturday dinner. It's easy to add another duck if there are even more of you eating.

1 duck
$^1/_2$ cucumber
6 spring onions
1 x 270ml jar Hoisin sauce

1 Preheat the oven to 170°C/gas mark 3.

2 Cut off the flap of fat that hangs over the duck's cavity. Sit the trimmed duck on a rack or slotted tray over a deep roasting tin and roast for 4 hours.

3 Increase the oven temperature to 220°C/gas mark 7 and give a final 30 minutes of intense heat. Or, if it's easier, just leave the duck in the low oven for $5^1/_2$ hours. The choice is yours.

4 Sit pancakes on the top part of a steamer to cook or simply follow the instructions on the packet.

5 Pour the Hoisin sauce into a bowl.

6 Cut the cucumber into matchsticks (like you get in a Chinese restaurant).

7 Cut the spring onions lengthways into short strips (again, as in Chinese restaurants).

9 Carefully take the duck, in its tin, out of the oven. Transfer the duck to a board, shred it, using two forks to pull the meat apart, and set it on the table with the sauce, pancakes, cucumber and spring onion shreds, so everyone can make their own pancake parcels. (When the duck fat has cooled a little, pour it into a bowl or jar, and save. It's great for frying potatoes.)

Serves 4–6

LAMB, OLIVE AND CARAMELIZED ONION TAGINE

Nearly all stews start with chopped onion. Here is the lazy person's version, which uses some caramelized onion out of a jar instead (though if you've made some of your own onion mush, see page 109, do use that). And I add to the desirable idleness by not even searing the meat. I just tip everything into a big pan and let it do its own sweet thing without any interference from me. I don't actually cook this in a tagine – though often serve it in one – but ever since someone told me that in Morocco most tagines are made in pressure cookers, I have felt unembarrassed by calling something cooked in a pan a tagine. And by all means use a pressure cooker if you're that way inclined. I've tried them, but always return to pots and pans that don't hiss at me.

I prefer to cook this in a low oven rather than on the hob, but a licking simmer would do as well. Like all stews, it benefits from being cooked in advance, so it makes sense to cook this on a day when you have the time, and eat it – reheating it on the hob, all of it, or in batches as suits – when you're in more of a hurry.

The quickest, and most suitable, accompaniment is a bowl of couscous, pale and plain or studded with a can or two of chickpeas.

1 x 1kg leg of lamb, diced	4 x 15ml tablespoons capers
1 head garlic, separated into cloves	2 teaspoons ground cumin
1 x 350g can pitted black olives in brine, to give 150g drained weight	2 teaspoons ground ginger
100g caramelized onions from a jar	1 x 75cl bottle red wine

1 Preheat the oven to 150°C/gas mark 2.

2 Put all the ingredients into a casserole or heavy-based pan, pouring in the wine last and giving everything a good stir.

3 Bring the pan to a boil, then clamp on the lid and put into the oven for 2 hours or until the lamb is very tender.

Serves 6–8

LAMB SHANKS WITH BEANS

The trouble with the sort of speedy cooking which can't help but be the mainstay of our daily repertoire is that it necessarily leaves out the food that makes you feel cosy rather than briskly efficient. But even if I know I've only got ten minutes of free time over two days, I can still make sure I get something big and bolstering on the table. On one day I stick my lamb shanks in to marinate, on the other I put them in the oven, leaving them there while I battle over homework or try to clear my desk or tackle whatever other doomed task I set myself.

The beans I'm happy to get out of a can. I love their pinks and browns and tones of Tuscan stone and they turn a pile of bones into a feast.

250ml white wine
4 x 15ml tablespoons redcurrant jelly, plus 1 teaspoon
2 x 15ml tablespoons Worcestershire sauce
60ml garlic oil, plus 2 x 15ml tablespoons
2 onions, quartered
1 x 10cm sprig rosemary or 1 teaspoon dried

6 lamb shanks
60ml water
1 x 15ml tablespoon Dijon mustard
4 x 400g cans mixed beans (sometimes sold as mixed bean salad)
salt and pepper to taste

1   Get out two freezer bags and divide the wine, the 4 tablespoons of redcurrant jelly, the Worcestershire sauce, 60ml of garlic oil, the onions and the rosemary between the two of them. Put 3 lamb shanks in each bag. Seal the bags and put in the fridge overnight, or for up to two days.

2   When the shanks have had their marinating time, take them out of the fridge and preheat the oven to 200°C/gas mark 6.

3   Tip the contents of the bags into a roasting tin and slot this in the oven, turning it down immediately to 170°C/gas mark 3. Roast for about an hour and a half, and then remove the shanks to a warmed serving dish.

4   In a pan big enough to hold the beans, warm the water, the remaining 2 tablespoons of garlic oil and Dijon mustard. Add the beans and heat gently, stirring occasionally with a wooden spatula. Season with salt and pepper to taste and then pour the contents of the pan into the dish containing the shanks.

5   Serve with more redcurrant jelly and perhaps a tomato salad alongside.

Serves 6

COQ AU RIESLING

I have always loved the Alsatian version of coq au vin and this is it in a stunningly stream-lined version. I replace the onion with leek, buy chicken thighs and ready-cubed lardons. The brown meat is always best in a stew. In fact, nearly always best full stop. I don't bother to sear the meat, which means you really need skinless portions; unbrowned chicken skin is not pretty. If you're not buying thighs, but thigh fillets, then it is probably more helpful to think in terms of boned weight, rather than the number of portions: go, here, for about 1.25 kilos.

I tend not to add any cream to this first time around but, if I have a small amount left over, I add a little double cream and turn it into a pasta sauce. I like to eat my coq au Riesling as they do in Alsace, with a huge pile of buttered noodles. Whether you add cream or not is entirely up to you.

2 x 15ml tablespoons garlic oil
150g bacon lardons
1 leek, finely sliced
12 boneless, skinless chicken thighs
3 bay leaves
300g oyster mushrooms, torn into
    strips

1 x 75cl bottle Riesling
double cream (optional)
salt and pepper to taste
1–2 tablespoons chopped fresh dill to
    serve

1   Heat the oil in a casserole or large, wide pan and fry the lardons until crisp.

2   Add the sliced leek and soften it with the lardons for a minute or so.

3   Cut chicken thighs into 2 or 3 pieces each, tip them into the pan with the bay leaves, torn mushrooms and wine.

4   Season with salt and pepper to taste and bring to the boil, cover the pan and simmer gently for 30–40 minutes, stirring in the double cream for the last couple of minutes if you want. Like all stews, this tastes its mellowest best if you let it get cold and then reheat the next day. But it's no hardship to eat straight off. Whichever, serve sprinkled with dill and together with some buttered noodles.

Serves 6

Swedish Salmon

I think of this as a curious amalgam of my two grandmothers. My maternal grand-mother was a passionate, if that is the right word to describe stirrings for the frozen north, espouser of all things Swedish – design, décor, dill. My paternal grandmother taught me to cook salmon this way, and there is no better. That's to say, you don't really cook it, you just get it hot and let it get cold over several hours – so this is one to make in advance. And I promise you, you have never tasted cold poached salmon till you have tasted it this way: its tender coral flesh is delicate but flavoursome and it makes cooking for a big crowd – think weekend lunch in summer – almost disconcertingly easy.

For me it has to be eaten with the mustardy dill sauce (though feel free to sub-stitute lemon or lime wedges), which is why I have merged the two recipes. Either way, sit the salmon on a plate lined with watercress or other peppery leaves, and I recommend serving with the Sweet and Sour Cucumber and Warm Potato salads that follow.

If it makes you feel more positive, believe me, you don't have to have any expe-rience of filleting fish. I find that, cooked like this, you can just lift up the tail end and start slicing, and the whole top fillet will come off in your hands; remove the backbone and you have the other fillet. But sometimes, I just cut pieces off, as I think they look better in (not huge) chunks on the plate.

1 salmon (preferably wild), weighing approx. 2.25kg, cleaned and scaled	1 teaspoon peppercorns
25g (small bunch) dill, plus 3 x 15ml tablespoons chopped dill	4 spring onions, whole
	3 x 15ml tablespoons Dijon mustard
2 x 15ml tablespoons Maldon salt plus 1 teaspoon, or 1 tablespoon table salt plus $^1/_2$ teaspoon	2 x 15ml tablespoons light brown sugar
	250ml sour cream
2 x 15ml tablespoons caster sugar	3 x 15ml tablespoons white wine vinegar

1　Lay the salmon in a flameproof roasting tin (or a fish kettle if you have one), cutting its head and/or tail off if necessary, and stuff the cavity with the bunch of dill.

2　Add the 2 tablespoons of salt, the caster sugar, peppercorns and spring onions to your tin, and pour over sufficient cold water to just cover the salmon.

3　Place on the heat and bring to the boil, then turn down to a gentle simmer, cover with foil and let bubble timidly for 10 minutes.

4　Remove the tin from the hob and turn the salmon over. Don't worry about ripping the skin as you will be filleting it later. Leave to get cold (this takes a while, so if you plan to eat it for supper, make it in the morning; if for lunch, do it the previous evening), cover-ing loosely with baking parchment or greaseproof paper.

5　When the water's cold, the salmon will be perfectly cooked and very, very succulent and tender.

6 Remove the salmon from its cold poaching liquid to a large piece of greaseproof paper or baking parchment. Take off the skin, and carefully cut fillets off the fish in whatever way is easiest for you.

7 Arrange on a serving place and get on with the sauce.

8 Whisk together the mustard and sugar, and then whisk in the sour cream and vinegar, the remaining salt to taste and, finally, the chopped dill. Transfer to a jug to serve alongside the salmon.

Serves 10–12

Sweet and Sour Cucumber Salad

I love this summer salad of Mitteleuropa. It is also unfathomably good with hot frankfurters. Even though it does get a little more watery, it is still fantastic after it's been sitting in the fridge for a while, which makes it another easy do-ahead dish. Just transfer it to a serving bowl with a spatula if need be.

2 medium-sized cucumbers
2 teaspoons caster sugar
2 x 15ml tablespoons white wine vinegar

2 teaspoons Maldon salt or
  1 teaspoon table salt
2 x 15ml tablespoons finely chopped fresh dill

1 Peel and finely slice the cucumbers into wafer-thin circles and transfer to a large bowl.

2 In a measuring jug, whisk the sugar, vinegar and salt and pour over the cucumbers, turning well to mix.

3 Add the chopped dill, toss again, and then turn into a shallow serving dish. Or else, cover with clingfilm and chill in the fridge until needed (up to 4 hours).

Serves 10–12

Warm Potato Salad

I have a difficulty with those potato salads that are claggy with mayo and which burn the oesophagus with too enthusiastic a scattering of raw onion. This is more my thing: no peeling – to start with – and then, finally, a sousing with white wine vinegar mixed with mustard and bacon. And the spring onions are gentle. I love it warm, but so long as you mix the dressing and the potatoes while they're themselves warm, it doesn't matter if you eat the salad cold. Or, rather, at room temperature: do not chill it in the fridge. And don't crumble the bacon over the salad until you're ready to serve it.

2kg baby new potatoes, scrubbed
4 spring onions, finely sliced
1 x 15ml tablespoon garlic oil
8 rashers bacon

1 x 15ml tablespoon wholegrain mustard
1–2 teaspoons white wine vinegar

1 Bring a pan of salted water to the boil and tip in the potatoes. Cook for 20 minutes or until tender, then drain and cut in half (if you can be bothered).

2 Put the potatoes into a large bowl and add the finely sliced spring onions.

3 Heat the oil in the warm potato pan and cook the bacon until really crispy, then remove to a plate.

4 Take off the heat and add the vinegar and mustard, give a little stir, then tip in the potatoes and spring onions and toss everything together before transferring to a serving bowl. You can leave it like this for an hour or so.

5 When you are ready to serve the salad, crumble most of the crisp bacon over it and toss again, then sprinkle with the remaining bits of bacon.

Serves 10–12

GRAVLAX SASHIMI

This was not intended to be the Swedish section of the book, but it occurred to me after making some gravlax a Christmas or so ago, that the method would be a very good way of curing a piece of salmon to create fear-free sashimi at home. Obviously, as well as having some Japanese flavours – the wasabi and saké, and no dill – this is a completely effort-free take on what can be a little fiddly.

You can buy the piece of salmon at the supermarket, along with the flavourings. Everything goes in a dish in the fridge and is just left there for 2–5 days.

It makes a different kind of supper and a very good one: you can eat it as if it were Scandinavian, along with rye bread and gherkins or as here, with more of a nod to its Japanese association, with sushi rice, pickled ginger and a blob or two of wasabi.

500g skinless salmon fillet, preferably organic
3 x 15ml tablespoons Maldon salt or 1¹/₂ x 15ml tablespoons table salt

3 x 15ml tablespoons caster sugar
1 x 15ml tablespoon wasabi
1¹/₂ x 15ml tablespoons saké

1   Put the salmon in a glass dish.

2   Mix the salt, sugar, wasabi paste and saké in a little bowl and smear half of it over the salmon. Turn the salmon over and smear over the rest.

3   Cover the dish with clingfilm, making sure you press down on the salmon and in the corners, before bringing it over and down the sides.

4   Place cans of beans or unopened jars of pickles on the salmon to weight it down, and put everything in the fridge for at least two days or up to five.

5   When you want to eat the salmon, remove it from the dish and wipe it with kitchen paper. Sit it on a board and cut down into strips and then cut each strip into two or three, to make sashimi-suitable shapes.

Serves 8

MOONBLUSH TOMATOES

I used to baulk at the "sunblush" tomatoes you can get at delis, the sort that are dried down to essence of tomato and steeped in oregano and oil. But I find them incredibly useful and disconcertingly good. I'd tried making my own, in the past, but even at the lowest possible heat, my oven seemed too hot for the job. Now, though, I've hit on the way, which is simply to put them in a very hot oven, turn it off and leave the tomatoes overnight; hence "moon" blush. I am addicted to making them now.

Feel free to substitute the homespun variety in any recipe that stipulates shop-bought sunblush (though I'd use about half; the shop ones are heavier per tomato) and I've put one of my favourite recipes for their usage below. Frankly, though they're wonderful eaten just as they are, with bread, cheese, or as a salad.

I also make them exactly the same way with large tomatoes, roughly chopped – and see them looking glorious with the tuna on page 151. This makes a fabulous instant pasta sauce, too.

500g (about 24) on-the-vine cherry or
    other baby tomatoes
2 teaspoons Maldon salt or
    1 teaspoon table salt

$^1/_4$ teaspoon sugar
1 teaspoon dried thyme
2 x 15ml tablespoons olive oil

1   Preheat the oven to 220°C/gas mark 7.

2   Cut the tomatoes in half and sit them cut side up in an ovenproof dish. Sprinkle with the salt, sugar, thyme and olive oil.

3   Put them in the oven, and immediately turn it off. Leave the tomatoes in the oven overnight or for a day without opening the door.

SLOW-ROAST TOMATOES, GOAT'S CHEESE AND MINT SALAD

200g rocket or spinach salad
2 x 100g tubs soft goat's cheese,
    such as Chavroux
1 batch moonblush tomatoes (see
    previous recipe)

1 x 15ml tablespoon lemon juice
2 x 15ml tablespoons extra virgin
    olive oil
2 x 15ml tablespoons chopped fresh
    mint

1   Arrange the salad leaves in a large dish and then scoop out spoonfuls of the soft goat's cheese and dollop it here and there.

2   Add the cooked-down, intensely red moonblush tomato halves.

3   In the same dish the tomatoes have been cooking in, whisk together the lemon juice and oil and pour over the salad.

4   Scatter with the chopped mint.

Serves 8

Lazy Loaf

It is heartening to know that you can be in a permanent hurry – and not spend more than a few minutes at any time anywhere, let alone in the kitchen – and still make a beautiful loaf of bread.

This is it – a few ingredients lazily stirred together in a bowl, and then put into a loaf tin in the oven. There is no kneading and proving. It feels like a cheat, but it isn't. It's the right, real thing.

200g best-quality oaty sugar-free
muesli (I like Rude Health's
Ultimate Muesli)
325g wholewheat bread flour
1 x 6g sachet easyblend yeast

2 teaspoons Maldon salt or
1 teaspoon table salt
250ml semi-skimmed milk
250ml water

1   Mix the muesli, flour, yeast and salt in a bowl and then pour in the milk and water and stir to mix. It will be like a thick porridge.

2   Transfer to a greased or silicone 900g loaf tin; actually, they're generally still sold as 2lb tins. Put this in a cold oven, turning it immediately on to 110°C/gas mark $^1/_4$ and leave for 45 minutes.

3   When these 45 minutes are up, turn the oven up to 180°C/gas mark 4 and leave for 1 hour, by which time the bread should be golden and cooked through. Slip it out of its tin and, although dense – it is that kind of loaf – it should feel slightly hollow when you knock it underneath. You can always slip it back in the oven, out of its tin, for a few minutes if you think it needs more.

4   Remove to a rack, and let cool.

No Churn Pomegranate Ice Cream

It's not hard to think of a pudding that can be made in advance. But mostly the advantage is simply that all the effort is upfront and early. The thing about this recipe is that you do it in advance – it's ice cream, so that stands to reason – but what you do in advance is negligible in terms of effort. You don't make a custard, and you don't have to keep whipping it out of the deep freeze to beat the crystals. No, you simply squeeze and stir.

On top of that cause for greater contentment, there is also the fact that this delicate pink ice cream tastes like fragrant, sherbety heaven.

2 pomegranates (plus seeds from a third for decoration, optional)
1 lime
175g icing sugar
500ml double cream

1   Juice the pomegranates and the lime and strain the juices into a bowl.

2   Add the icing sugar and whisk to dissolve.

3   Whisk in the double cream and keep whisking until soft peaks form in the pale pink cream.

4   Spoon and smooth the ice cream into the airtight container of your choice and freeze for at least 4 hours, or overnight.

5   Scatter with some pomegranate seeds before you eat it.

Serves 8

Irish Cream Tiramisu

I've long been tinkering about with a bottle of Baileys, seeing how it could best be called upon in the kitchen, and I think, with this, I've found it. An Italian friend of mine, who makes a killer tiramisu herself, was an instant convert. I was relieved: the Italians generally are conservative about their food, which goes some way to explaining the longevity of their cherished culinary traditions. But this only sounds like some sort of joke – "Did you hear the one about the Irishman and the Italian . . .?" – and in reality is an elegantly buff-tinted, creamy-toned variant of the punchy, if comfortably clichéd, original.

350ml espresso coffee, made with
   350ml water and 9 teaspoons
   instant espresso powder, cooled
250ml Baileys cream liqueur
2 x 200g packets Savoiardi (Italian
   lady finger) biscuits

2 eggs
75g caster sugar
500g mascarpone
2$\frac{1}{2}$ teaspoons cocoa powder

1   Mix the coffee with 175ml of the Baileys in a shallow bowl.

2   Dip the biscuits into this liquid; let them soak on each side enough to become damp but not soggy. Line the bottom of a 22cm square glass dish with a layer of biscuits.

3   Separate the eggs, but keep only one of the whites. Whisk the two yolks and the sugar together until thick and a paler yellow, then fold in the remaining 75ml of Baileys, and the mascarpone to make a moussy mixture.

4   Whisk the single egg white until thick and frothy; you can do this by hand with such a little amount. Fold the egg white into the yolky mascarpone, and then spread half of this mixture on top of the layer of biscuits.

5   Repeat with another layer of soaked Savoiardi, and then top with the remaining mascarpone mixture.

6   Cover the dish with clingfilm and leave in the fridge overnight. When you are ready to serve, push the cocoa powder through a small tea strainer to dust the top of the tiramisu.

Serves 12, though it doesn't have to …

FORGOTTEN PUDDING

There is a wonderful poetry to the name of this pudding which, thankfully, once eaten could never be forgotten. It's an old, old recipe popularly exhumed – I believe – by the late, great Richard Sax. Think of it as a kind of marshmallow-based pavlova. That's to say, you whip egg whites as if making meringue, spread on a swiss roll tin (or that's how I make it) and put in an oven which – as with the Moonblush Tomatoes on page 126 – you immediately switch off, leaving the pudding to cook overnight, hence "forgotten".

As for the yolks you discard: add a couple of whole eggs to them and make an intensely golden version of the Mexican Scrambled Eggs on page 230.

6 egg whites	butter for greasing
$^1/_2$ teaspoon salt	250ml double cream
250g caster sugar, plus 2 teaspoons	4 passionfruit
$^1/_2$ teaspoon cream of tartar	175g blackberries
1 teaspoon vanilla extract	175g strawberries, quartered

1 Preheat the oven to 220°C/gas mark 7.

2 In a large bowl, whisk the egg whites and salt until peaks begin to form.

3 Gradually add the 250g of sugar, then the cream of tartar and vanilla, whisking all the while at speed, until the whites are stiff and glossy.

4 Butter a swiss roll tin then spread evenly with the meringue mixture.

5 Put in the oven, close the door, then immediately switch off the oven and leave overnight, without opening the door or even thinking of peeking.

6 When you want to serve it, remove to a large plate.

7 Whisk the double cream until thick but still soft and spread over the marshmallow-meringue.

8 Scoop out the seeds and pulp of the passionfruit and dot them over the cream. Tumble the blackberries over the top. Toss the quartered strawberries in the remaining 2 teaspoons of caster sugar and arrange them on the cream, too.

9 Cut into slices; I cut 3 down and 2 across to make 12 squares.

Makes 12

Against the clock

One of the oft-cited laments of those who don't really enjoy cooking is that a meal takes so much less time to eat than it does to cook. I don't mind that, not least because I always relish a bit of pottering about in the kitchen; it's the only time I ever get to myself. But also, I confess to an affinity with that Victorian worldview, the constant harping on the inevitability of decline – "the woods decay, the woods decay and fall", that sort of thing – and the reminders that all things go back into the earth or up to the heavens. I don't resist the implacable cycle of meals, the kitchen grind.

Luckily, enough of my life is spent on what feels like some sort of cake-walk treadmill for me to have sympathy with those who have a less sentimental attachment to both the kitchen and my fond futilism. There are days, and probably those days are in the majority, when I feel I have no more than 10 minutes to get supper on the table. Yes, I am willing every now and again to have bread and cheese. I love bread and cheese. But most days I want a proper supper. And I mean "proper". I am not interested in making something easy but dispiriting to eat: as far as I'm concerned every eating opportunity has to be relished, and the idea of wasting one by eating something I don't really want or that doesn't give me pleasure is too hideous to contemplate. It happens, but I am inconsolable afterwards.

Actually, I eat so fast that I'd have thought it would be impossible for me ever to find any recipe that takes less time to cook than to eat, but desperate times call for desperate measures – and if an exhausted weeknight, after a six o'clock meeting, a row over homework and a reproachful list of unreturned phone calls and emails doesn't count as desperate times, I don't know what does. I need food I can cook fast or else – not least – I'll eat too much while I'm waiting for supper to be ready. Cook, feed thyself. And indeed I do, on the sorts of foods that follow. These are recipes that are almost too bare-bones to be called that, using ingredients that need at most a quick blitz in a hot pan or a basic, effortless warm-through. They're my fast fall-backs, the sort of meals I can cook when I'm squeezed for time at every angle. In other words, you can do a supermarket sweep at lunch and snatch yourself supper in the evening. And, what's more, the washing up's minimal too.

Flash-Fried Steak with White Bean Mash

When I was a child, steak houses always had something called minute steak – as in *minnit* – on the menu, economically attractive portions that needed a mere 60 seconds to cook through. In our house they were pronounced *mynewt* steaks, as if in baffled disappointment at the meagreness of the meat provided. It's hard to throw off the idea that a steak should be something chunky and big enough to get your teeth into and I certainly like my meat rare. When I'm asked in a restaurant how I want my steak cooked, I tell them just to hit it on the head and walk it straight through. So I can do a proper, fleshly steak supper pretty damn fast, but when you're really up against it, this is the perfect almost-instant dinner. Under five minutes is what I'm talking about from start to finish – and that isn't bad. I could hone it down by sticking to the minute steak idea, and it's fine, only there's something a little school dinners about those sad little straggly rags of steam.

This is my compromise: a slender but still substantial steak that cooks for 90 seconds a side. And in that time, I've produced a garlicky, lemony, ultra-fabulous, utterly addictive bean mash. Below makes enough for four, more if that includes children, but I have to come clean and say that I don't quite halve the amounts for the mash when there are just two of us eating. This is just too good, and I simply go down to 2 cans of beans and a little less of everything else. I'm afraid I don't really want to reduce anything at all.

60ml olive oil, plus 2 teaspoons	3 x 410g cans white beans
most of 1 clove garlic, crushed	4 thin-cut sirloin or entrecôte steaks,
1 sprig fresh rosemary, optional	about 150g each
grated zest and juice of 1 lemon	salt to taste

1   First, get on with the beans: put the 60ml of olive oil in a saucepan, and mix in the garlic. Add the whole rosemary sprig, if using, and the lemon zest and warm through. Remove the rosemary, but do not throw away.

2   Drain the beans and rinse under a tap to get rid of the gloop and then add to the pan and warm through, stirring and squishing with a wide, flat spoon so that the beans go into a nobbly mush. Season to taste; some beans come saltier than others.

3   Meanwhile, heat a teaspoon of oil in a large frying pan and cook the steaks on high for a minute and a half a side. Remove to warmed plates, sprinkling some salt, to taste, over them as you do so.

4   Squeeze the lemon juice into the hot pan and let it bubble up with the meaty oil, then pour over the steaks. Serve immediately with the bean mash adorned with the reserved rosemary sprig.

Serves 4

Chicken Schnitzel with Bacon and White Wine

It stands to reason that if you want food to cook quickly it needs, first of all, to be fit for purpose. Thin cuts of meat – and, indeed, fish – are obvious contenders here, but you do have to make sure that speed doesn't take priority over taste. A chicken schnitzel, or escalope, plain grilled, is certainly fast fare, but it wouldn't make you skip to the dinner table. Bacon comes to the rescue here; nothing fancy, just sweet, salty ribbons from Oscar Meyer which I always keep in the fridge for just such an eventuality.

There's something about the coming together of bacon and white wine that is simple – but ever-compelling. For me, it's the smell, the lure, of carbonara and what it does here is ooze its way through the pan-scorched chicken to make this feel like a treat. And if you can do that with a boneless, skinless piece of chicken breast, you're doing something right.

I love this with some fine green beans – even my children do – and if you have any schnitzel left over, chop it up and heat with a little cream and Parmesan to make a quick pasta sauce.

1 teaspoon garlic oil	4 chicken escalopes approx. 125g each
4 rashers streaky bacon	100ml white wine

AGAINST THE CLOCK

1 Put the oil in a frying pan and add the bacon.

2 Fry till the bacon is crisp and the pan is full of bacony juices. Remove the bacon to a piece of foil, wrap it and set it aside for a moment.

3 Fry the chicken for about 2 minutes a side, until there is no pinkness when you cut into a piece. Make sure the pan's hot so that the escalopes catch a little, turning beautifully bronze.

4 Remove the chicken to a serving plate and quickly crumble the bacon you've set aside into the pan, then pour in the wine, letting everything bubble up, and, finally, pour over the chicken pieces.

Serves 4

High-Speed Hamburger with Fast Fries

I adore a proper burger, but it does need to be a proper one. And although I've been successful at various versions, I've never made one that has been either quick or very convincing-looking. Luckily, my love of gadgetry, combined with my catalogue-compulsion, led to this: the perfect burger, in record time. I use something called, straightforwardly, a burger press. You line it with a little disc of waxed paper (these discs come with it) and then put in your 125g of meat, put another disc on top, and press. You will not believe how much it makes you want to work in a burger factory.

I always thought that lean meat made tough burgers, but after much experimentation, I found that the best meat for burgers is that sold as "extra lean", which means that it has, typically, a mere 5% fat. I use Aberdeen Angus or organic beef.

The fast fries are not as professional looking as the burgers, but are every bit as satisfying to make. They certainly help you rid yourself of the day's aggro.

AGAINST THE CLOCK

250g extra lean minced beef
1 x 15ml tablespoon caramelized onions from a jar
1^1/$_2$ teaspoons buttermilk or natural yogurt

1^1/$_2$ teaspoons soy sauce
1^1/$_2$ teaspoons Worcestershire sauce
good grinding of pepper
vegetable oil for brushing

1 Mix the minced beef with the onions, buttermilk, soy sauce and Worcestershire sauce, season with pepper, and divide into two portions. Put each in turn into the burger press, or shape them by hand.

2 Heat a ridged griddle pan and lightly brush the burgers with oil. Cook the burgers for 2 minutes on the first side, and then flip them and cook for another minute. Remove and stand for a minute or two; this will give you medium-rare burgers.

3 Serve with the fast fries and sandwich in a toasted bun, if you wish. Add salad, melted blue cheese and bacon or a fried, poached or squished soft boiled egg, as you like.

Fast Fries

250g new potatoes, scrubbed   60ml vegetable oil

1 Place the potatoes in a freezer bag and hit them with a rolling pin until they are broken into pieces.

2 Heat the oil in a frying pan and, when hot, add the potatoes and cook for 5–6 minutes a side with the pan partially covered.

3 Remove the potatoes to a plate lined with kitchen paper.

Serves 2

GAMMON STEAKS WITH PARSLEY

Of course, I'm tempted to do a gammon steak with pineapple, and I wouldn't begin to stop you, but I think parsley is really the key here. When I've got time, I am happy to stand at the hob, whisking up a roux, and stirring, stirring, stirring to usher forth the perfect velvety parsley sauce, but a quick flick of parsley in a pan works in a more sprightly way.

I'm all for peas as an accompaniment, and keep a stash of frozen ones at the ready. Nevertheless, it's hard for me to forswear a can of luridly green marrowfat peas here. Yes, they are processed and I'd prefer not to read the ingredients list on the back of the can, but I can't help loving them. A can or jar of those small, grey-green French peas would be an excellent substitute for those not sharing my low tastes. Or cook and drain some frozen peas, blending them with a little Parmesan, pepper and mascarpone.

2 teaspoons garlic oil	lots of freshly ground pepper
2 gammon steaks, approx. 200g each	2 teaspoons honey
2 x 15ml tablespoons white wine vinegar	4 x 15ml tablespoons roughly chopped parsley
4 x 15ml tablespoons water	

Against the Clock

1 Heat the garlic oil in a large-ish, heavy-based frying pan and, when hot, add the gammon steaks and cook for about 3 minutes a side. Remove to two warmed dinner plates.

2 Take the pan off the heat. Whisk the vinegar with the water, pepper and honey and quickly throw into the (still hot) pan along with most of the parsley. Swirl, stir and scrape to mix, and then pour over the gammon steaks.

3 Add the vegetable of your choice, and sprinkle the rest of the parsley over the two plates of food before tucking in.

Serves 2

Mirin-Glazed Salmon

This must be the fastest way there is to create a culinary sensation. You do scarcely a thing – just dibble some salmon steaks in a dark glossy potion, most of which you get out of a jar – and what you make tastes as if you had been dedicating half your life to achieving the perfect combination of sweet, savoury, tender and crisp.

If there are only two of you eating, I would be inclined to stick to the quantities given here, letting a couple of pieces or whatever you don't eat get cold, as it makes a fantastic salad the next day.

My favourite accompaniment here is sushi rice, and since I am wedded to my rice cooker, this is no work and needs no skill whatsoever. Just cook rice of your choice – or noodles if you prefer – according to the instructions on the packet if, cruelly, you are rice-cookerless.

60ml mirin (Japanese sweet rice wine)
50g light brown sugar
60ml soy sauce
4 x 125g pieces salmon, cut from the
   thick part of the fillet so that they
   are narrow but tall rather than
   wide and flat

2 x 15ml tablespoons rice vinegar
1–2 spring onions, halved and
   shredded into fine strips

1 Mix the mirin, brown sugar and soy sauce in a shallow dish that will take all 4 pieces of salmon, and marinate the salmon in it for 3 minutes on the first side and 2 minutes on the second. Meanwhile heat a large non-stick frying pan on the hob.

2 Cook the salmon in the hot, dry pan for 2 minutes and then turn the salmon over, add the marinade and cook for another 2 minutes.

3 Remove the salmon to whatever plate you're serving it on, add the rice vinegar to the hot pan, and warm through.

4 Pour the dark, sweet, salty glaze over the salmon and top with the spring onion strips. Serve with rice or noodles as you wish, and consider putting some sushi ginger on the table, too.

Serves 4

Tuna Steaks with Black Beans

Fresh tuna is good only when it's scarcely, if at all, cooked; once its Carpaccio red flesh turns to that grey mauve, it's not dinner you have in front of you, but a disaster. This, of course, works to our advantage here, as speed is what we're after. Indeed, it takes marginally longer to open a can of beans, drain them and douse them in dressing than it does to cook the fish. Some tomato salad always works, too; here I've spooned up some leftover Moonblush Tomatoes (see pag 126), of the roughly chopped rather than cherry-halved variety.

It's not surprising, then, that I make this very, very often for supper. I get the tuna steaks during my weekly assault on the supermarket and feel just that little bit calmer the minute they're safely in my fridge.

2 teaspoons lime juice
1 teaspoon fish sauce (nam pla)
2 teaspoons chilli oil
1 teaspoon honey
1 x 400g can black beans

2 x 15ml tablespoons chopped fresh coriander
2 thin-cut tuna steaks, approx. 125g each
$^1/_2$ teaspoon Maldon salt

1 Heat a ridged griddle pan and, while it's heating up, prepare the black bean salad.

2 In a bowl, whisk the lime juice, fish sauce, chilli oil and honey.

3 Drain the beans and rinse them to remove any gloop, then toss them in the dressing to coat well. Add most of the coriander and divide between two dinner plates.

4 Slap the tuna steaks on the griddle and cook for 30 seconds a side. If the steaks are not very thin, you may want to give them another 30 seconds each side; cut into one to check that it's cooked as you like it, before placing the tuna on the plate with the beans, adding tomatoes or any other salad you like. Sprinkle the tuna steaks with some coarse salt (not table salt).

Serves 2

SCALLOPS AND CHORIZO

I've long been a fan of scallops with bacon, and scallops with chilli, and this is my combination of the two, using chorizo – the sausage, not the salami – to ooze its paprika-hot orange oil over the sweet, white scallops. It's quicker than the speed of light to make and quite as dazzling.

110g chorizo sausage
400g small scallops (halve them to make 2 thinner discs if they are very fat)
juice of $^1/_2$ lemon
4 x 15ml tablespoons chopped fresh parsley

1 Slice the chorizo into rounds no thicker than 3mm.

2 Heat a heavy-based pan on the hob and, when hot, dry-fry the chorizo round until crisped on either side (the chorizo will give out plenty of its own oil); this should take no more than 2 minutes.

3 Remove the chorizo to a bowl and fry the scallops in the chorizo-oil for about 1 minute a side.

4 Return the chorizo to the pan with the scallops, add the lemon juice and let bubble for a few seconds before arranging on a serving plate and sprinkling with lots of parsley.

Serves 4 as a main course with the Chickpeas with Rocket and Sherry overleaf; 8 as a starter with a little leafage

CHICKPEAS WITH ROCKET AND SHERRY

This is not quite a stir-fry, though I do cook it in my wok. The chickpeas get soused with the sherry and infused with cumin, and the rocket, or rather the tangle of green things that come in the packet called "roquette salad" at my supermarket, wilt leggily in the pan. This turns the chorizo and scallops into a feistily elegant main course, and is a useful way of providing a quick, filling bowl of not-the-usual vegetables whenever you want a boost.

1 x 15 ml tablespoon wok oil
2 teaspoons cumin seeds
2 x 410g cans chickpeas, drained and
   rinsed

1 x 130g packet roquette salad
1 teaspoon Maldon salt or
   $^1/_2$ teaspoon table salt
60ml cream sherry

1 Heat the oil and cumin seeds in a wok.

2 Add the chickpeas, salad, salt and sherry and give a good stir. Continue stirring over heat until the rocket and any other leaves have wilted, the chickpeas have warmed through and the liquid has reduced a little.

Serves 4 as a side dish; 2 as a main course with or without a poached or squished soft boiled egg each on top

Nectarine and Blueberry Galette

A galette is just a fancy way of saying "this is a pie, but don't get your hopes up". Not that this isn't good – it's very good indeed – but it is not a perfect specimen. In a way, its raw materials are not so very different from the Tarte Fine aux Pommes on page 217, but whereas there everything is orderly, here it's all thrown together. Suits me.

1 x approx. 375g sheet (40 x 23cm) all-butter shop-bought ready-rolled puff pastry, defrosted if frozen

2 x 15ml tablespoons apricot conserve or low-sugar jam

2 x 15ml tablespoons double cream

1 nectarine, cut into 16 segments

125g blueberries

2 teaspoons Demerara sugar

1 Preheat the oven to 220°C/gas mark 7.

2 Lay the puff pastry sheet out on a lined baking sheet and, using the point of a sharp knife, score a frame around the edge, about 2cm in from the edge.

3 In a small bowl mix together the apricot conserve and cream and paint or spread this on the pastry within the frame.

4 Arrange the fruit on top and sprinkle with Demerara sugar before baking for 15 minutes.

5 Cut into slices and eat while still warm.

Makes 6–8 pieces

INSTANT CHOCOLATE MOUSSE

Normally, you need to make chocolate mousse a good few hours, or better still a day, before you want to eat it, so that the egg yolk sets and the whisked whites permeate everything with air bubbles. Forget that: here we have no yolks, no whites, no whisking, no waiting.

Lack of raw egg, incidentally, also means that you might be happier giving this mousse to small children, though I certainly feel they shouldn't be the only beneficiaries.

150g mini marshmallows
50g soft butter
250g good dark chocolate (minimum 70% cocoa solids), chopped into small pieces

60ml hot water from a recently boiled kettle
1 x 284ml tub double cream
1 teaspoon vanilla extract

1 Put the marshmallows, butter, chocolate and water in a heavy-based saucepan.

2 Put the saucepan on the hob, over heat, though keep it fairly gentle, to melt the contents, stirring every now and again. Remove from the heat.

3 Meanwhile, whip the cream with the vanilla extract until thick, and then fold into the cooling chocolate mixture until you have a smooth, cohesive mixture.

4 Pour or scrape into 4 glasses or ramekins, about 175ml each in capacity, or 6 smaller (125ml) ones, and chill until you want to eat. The sooner the better!

Serves 4–6

CHOCOLATE PEANUT BUTTER FUDGE SUNDAE

I've saved this to last, and for good reason: it is the ultimate ice cream sundae. Obviously, if you're not a peanut-eater, it won't be for you, but for everyone else it is the stuff of dreams. Last time I made this sauce, I nearly had to make another batch, I'd eaten so much before even getting the ice creams out of the freezer.

Talking of which, obviously you should choose whichever flavours of ice cream you want. Even if you are reduced to just plain-old, same-old vanilla, you have a party right here. And you should know that the sauce is just as irresistible as a storecupboard special, if you replace the double cream and the syrup with half a can (200ml) sweetened condensed milk, whisking in an espresso cup of hot water from the kettle before pouring the glossy sauce out of the pan.

I made a jar of this for a friend to take home for her supper recently. As soon as she'd had it she sent a text saying, "Bottle that sauce, make millions". Well maybe, but until then, here's the recipe.

175ml double cream
100g milk chocolate, chopped
100g smooth peanut butter (Skippy
   for preference)
3 x 15ml tablespoons golden syrup
4 scoops toffee or caramel ice cream

4 scoops chocolate ice cream
4 scoops vanilla ice cream
4 x 15ml tablespoons salted peanuts,
   roughly chopped or left whole to
   taste

1 Put all the cream, chopped chocolate, peanut butter and golden syrup into a saucepan and place on the heat to melt, stirring occasionally. In about 2 minutes you should have your sauce ready.

2 Get out four sundae glasses and put a scoop of toffee or caramel ice cream in each, followed by one of chocolate and then another of vanilla.

3 Pour some chocolate peanut butter fudge sauce over each sundae and sprinkle with the salted peanuts. Hand them round and wait for people to weep with gratitude.

Serves 4 very lucky people

INSTANT CALMER

Although I know, from sad experience, that comfort eating does not rely on lengthy preparations, but rather a frenzied assault on the fridge, it cannot easily be rushed. A few ingredients, thrown together in spirited fashion, can make a fabulous supper, but this does not guarantee the enveloping cosiness we are sometimes hungry for. Nevertheless, I can't ignore the genre; it plays too important a part in life.

It's not hard to think up instant-eating ideas – warm toast, spread with too much butter and a sprinkling of cinnamon and sugar; a family-sized bar of milk chocolate; ice cream straight from the tub; canned rice pudding – but the solace they seem to promise is elusive, and one generally ends up hating oneself and feeling sick into the bargain. I want comfort food that really does comfort, that feeds me after a long, difficult day and helps me feel good about life rather than making me want to escape from it.

This, anyway, is the aim. But, yes, I do know that some of the recipes that follow are precisely for the sorts of food that I couldn't argue into any kind of diet plan organized by the healthy eating brigade. I can't defend my doughnut French toast from a nutritional point of view, certainly, but I know it has to exist.

These are recipes for the world as it is, for us as we are. I can't always be worrying about how we should be living or eating. I'm hungry now.

CHOWDER WITH ASIAN FLAVOURS

This is the perfect supper on those days when a knife and fork seem like just too much work. It's instantly comforting but spirited enough to make one feel invigorated rather than stultified by eating it. And although, to many, replacing the regular milk with coconut milk, dispensing with the flour and butter – the roux – altogether and taking the south east Asian route rather than the traditional one, might seem an abomination, I love it so much better than the anyway-more-laborious-to-prepare original.

Children may prefer the lime juice reduced and the chilli removed. I think it is perfection as it is.

750ml chicken stock (not instant)
500g baking potatoes or 2 medium-sized, peeled and cut into 5mm cubes
100g baby leeks, cut into 1cm slices
125g baby corn, cut into 5mm slices
2 bay leaves
1 teaspoon ground mace
1 x 400ml can coconut milk
600g skinless smoked cod fillets, cut into 2.5cm cubes

60ml lime juice
250g small or medium frozen prawns
300g canned sweetcorn, drained
1 teaspoon Maldon salt or
   $^1/_2$ teaspoon table salt
1 long red chilli, deseeded and finely chopped
20g fresh coriander, finely chopped

1   Bring the stock to the boil in a medium-sized pan. Cook the chopped potatoes, leeks and baby corn in the stock with the bay leaves and mace for about 10 minutes or until tender.

2   Add the coconut milk, chopped smoked fish and the lime juice. Bring the pan back to the boil and let it simmer for a minute or so.

3   Tip in the prawns and sweetcorn and once again let it come back to the boil to heat them through. Season with the salt and then serve.

4   Decorate each bowl with some chopped chilli and pungent, leafy coriander.

Serves 4

Noodle Soup for Needy People

I have to say, to be prescriptive about a noodle soup seems to be against the ethos of what you're actually cooking. When I need a noodle soup, believe me I am in no mood to start weighing and measuring. I heat some stock, of some description or other, and throw in a variety of vegetables that are skulking about in the fridge and the most soothing noodles I can find. You can add other things – some chicken strips or, at the end, some fine rags of raw tuna or salmon – but I generally want the vegetably broth and noodles by themselves. The protein element, while desirable in so many ways, I'm sure, is not what I'm after.

But anyway, I throw down a blueprint here. Don't get caught up in it, but follow if it feels helpful.

175g udon noodles (dried, from a packet)
750ml chicken or vegetable or dashi stock
1 teaspoon soft dark sugar
1 star anise
1 teaspoon crushed ginger

2 x 15ml tablespoons soy sauce
75g beansprouts
75g sugar-snap peas
75g sliced shitake mushrooms
2 heads baby pak choi, finely sliced
2 tablespoons chopped fresh coriander

1 Cook the noodles according to the packet instructions and, while their water is boiling, fill a nearby saucepan with the stock, sugar, star anise, crushed ginger and the soy sauce. (When the noodles are done, just drain them and divide between 2 serving bowls.)

2 When the flavoured stock comes to the boil, add the vegetables. They should be cooked before 2 minutes are up.

3 Pour half into each bowl, over the cooked and drained noodles, and sprinkle with the coriander.

Serves 2 for supper

BUTTERNUT AND SWEET POTATO SOUP

Ever since I overcame my prejudices about buying pre-chopped fruit and veg, my cooking life has got a lot simpler. And you should know that in Italian markets, storeholders regularly sell peeled and prepared vegetables bagged up to make their customers' life easier.

These squash and sweet potato dice certainly work for me; a quarter of an hour's bubbling with some stock and some spice, and sweet succour is to hand. Sometimes you are not in the mood to wait.

350g diced butternut squash and
    sweet potato from a packet
750ml hot chicken or vegetable stock
$^1/_4$ teaspoon ground cinnamon

$^1/_4$ teaspoon ground mace
good grinding of pepper
4 teaspoons buttermilk

1 Put the diced butternut and sweet potato in a saucepan with the hot chicken or vegetable stock and both spices.

2 Bring to the boil and simmer for 15 minutes, or until the vegetables are tender. Add some pepper to taste.

3 Purée the soup in a blender – you will find that by removing the centre nozzle on the lid and placing a hand or tea towel over the top, you will not get a build-up of pressure or an explosion of soup on your walls.

4 Pour the blended soup into two bowls, garnishing each bowl with swirls made with 2 teaspoons of buttermilk.

Serves 2, or 1 in great need of solace

INSTANT
CALMER

Rib-Sticking Stir-Fry

It's absolutely true that throwing everything in a wok can be a very quick way to get supper on the table, but there are times when what's wanted is something altogether more substantial than the virtuously oriental culinary traditions allow. There is a good amount of meat in this – either turkey or chicken, I use both interchangeably – and I bung in a can of cannellini beans rather than going to the, admittedly not really demanding, lengths of cooking and draining some noodles and throwing them in. Curiously it works. But then, food that can be eaten out of a bowl, with a spoon, always offers succour.

2 x 15ml tablespoons wok oil
300g chicken or turkey breast fillet,
   cut into 4cm x 0.5cm strips
300g stir-fry chopped vegetables
   (from a packet)

60ml soy sauce
60ml Chinese cooking wine
1 x 400g can cannellini beans, drained
1 x 15ml tablespoon chopped fresh
   coriander or parsley

1   Heat the oil in a wok, and, over a fairly high heat add the chicken or turkey strips and toss them until about to colour.

2   Once the meat has sealed, add the chopped vegetables and toss around again until they begin to soften, then add the soy sauce and the cooking wine. The soy sauce will help the meat strips bronze beautifully.

3   Once the heat is back up and sizzling, add the drained beans and toss everything about to mix before tipping onto two plates.

4   Sprinkle with the herbs and serve straight away.

Serves 2

Rapid Ragù

Much to my husband's horror, when I am feeling fragile and in need of cosiness and comfort, my favourite supper is a helping of minced meat with some grated cheese on top, eaten by greedy, grateful spoonful out of a cereal bowl.

I have dispensed with much of the usual, necessary chopping: I use cubes of pancetta (or *cubetti di pancetta*, as they're sold at my local supermarket) and a little caramelized onion from a jar. This is everything you could hope for, sweetly salving and as undemanding to make as it is rewarding to eat.

2 x 15ml tablespoons garlic oil
125g cubed pancetta
500g lamb mince
75g caramelized onions
80ml Marsala

1 x 400g can chopped tomatoes
75g green lentils
125ml water
50g grated red Leicester or Cheddar
(optional)

1 Heat the oil in a wide, medium-sized saucepan, and fry the cubed pancetta until beginning to crisp.

2 Add the lamb, breaking it up with a fork in the bacony pan as it browns.

3 Tip in the caramelized onions, Marsala, tomatoes, lentils and water and bring the pan to the boil.

4 Simmer the ragù for 20 minutes stirring occasionally. Sprinkle with the cheese (if using) before serving.

Serves 4

CHICKEN, MUSHROOM AND BACON PIE

Even the word pie is comforting. But then, it would be hard to deny the very real lure of pastry, especially when, as here, you know you're going to dunk it in gravied juices till its luscious lightness has become deliciously, soggily heavy. I concede, however, that making and rolling out your own pastry is not necessarily the speediest option, so I use bought, all-butter ready-rolled puff pastry and feel fine about it.

I make the pie even easier, by browning the chicken and making the sauce all in one go. And gold-crusted, welcoming pies for two people in half an hour is not bad going.

3 rashers streaky bacon, cut or scissored into 2.5cm strips	25g flour
1 teaspoon garlic oil	$1/2$ teaspoon dried thyme
125g chestnut mushrooms, sliced into 5mm pieces	1 x 15ml tablespoon butter
250g chicken thigh fillets cut into 2.5cm pieces	300ml hot chicken stock
	1 x 15ml tablespoon Marsala
	1 x 375g (23 x 40cm) sheet all-butter ready-rolled puff pastry

1　Preheat the oven to 220°C/gas mark 7. In a heavy-based frying pan, fry the bacon strips in the oil until beginning to crisp, then add the sliced mushrooms and soften them in the pan with the bacon.

2　Turn the chicken strips in the flour and thyme (you could toss them about in a freezer bag), and then melt the butter in the bacon-and-mushroom pan before adding the floury chicken and all the flour left in the bag. Stir around with the bacon and mushrooms until the chicken begins to colour.

3　Pour in the hot stock and Marsala, stirring to form a sauce, and let this bubble away for about 5 minutes.

4　Take two 300ml pie-pots (if yours are deeper, don't worry, there will simply be more space between contents and puff pastry top) and make a pastry rim for each one – by this I mean an approx. 1cm strip curled around the top of each pot. Dampen the edges with a little water to make the pastry stick.

5　Cut a circle bigger than the top of each pie-pot for the lid, and then divide the chicken filling between the two pots.

6　Dampen the rim of the pastry again and then pop on the lid of each pie, sealing the edges with your fingers or the underneath of the prongs of a fork.

7　Cook the pies for about 20 minutes turning them around halfway through cooking. Once cooked, they should have puffed up magnificently.

Serves 2

CHEDDAR CHEESE RISOTTO

This is the first of my holy trinity of cheese-rich comfort foods. There is just something about melted cheese, that perfect goo, which seems to soothe the soul and bolster the body.

This might seem odd to Italians (one of the reasons it's not in the Hey Presto chapter) but it works beautifully: the starchy rice, the sharp Cheddar, both are the perfect counterpoint for each other.

I make this on days when I need to escape to the kitchen and have a good, quiet, relaxing and mindless 20 minutes staring into the middle distance and stirring. I heartily recommend it.

1 x 15ml tablespoon butter
1 x 15ml tablespoon oil
2 baby leeks (or fat spring onions), finely sliced
300g risotto rice
125ml white wine

$^1/_2$ teaspoon Dijon mustard
1 litre hot vegetable stock
125g Cheddar, chopped
2 x 15ml tablespoons chopped fresh chives

1 Melt the butter and oil in a medium-sized pan and cook the sliced baby leeks until they have softened.

2 Add the risotto rice and keep stirring for a minute or so, then turn up the heat and add the wine and mustard, stirring until the wine is absorbed.

3 Start ladling in the hot stock, letting each ladleful become absorbed as you stir, before adding the next one.

4 Stir and ladle until the rice is al dente, about 18 minutes, then add the cheese, stirring it into the rice until it melts.

5 Take the pan straight off the heat, still stirring as you do so, and spoon the risotto into warmed dishes, sprinkling with some of the chopped chives.

Serves 2 as a main course; 4 as a starter

Macaroni Cheese

How could I have a chapter on comfort food without a recipe for macaroni cheese? But I knew there was a fundamental flaw: making a roux and a white sauce, for the base, is not everyone's idea of having a relaxing time; I realise that my regularly self-administered stirring-treatment is not for everyone.

This, then, is the shortcut version: no cheese sauce, but a gorgeously huge amount of cheese, bound with egg and evaporated milk. Yum.

250g macaroni
250g mature Cheddar or red Leicester
    or a mixture of both
250ml evaporated milk

2 eggs
grating of fresh nutmeg
salt and pepper

1 Preheat the oven to 220°C/gas mark 7. Cook the macaroni according to the packet instructions, drain and then put back into the hot pan.

2 While the pasta is cooking, put the cheese, evaporated milk, eggs and nutmeg in a processor and blitz to mix. Or grate the cheese and mix everything by hand.

3 Pour the cheese sauce over the macaroni, stir well, and season with salt and pepper to taste.

4 Tip into a 25.5cm-diameter dish (wide and shallow is best) and bake in the very hot oven for about 10–15 minutes, or until it is bubbling and blistering on top.

Serves 4

GRILLED CHEESE AND SLAW

By grilled cheese, of course, I mean a grilled cheese sandwich – a toastie in fact – and I add the slaw, both because I love it and because, that way, I don't feel so bad about making this for supper. And that's what works for me. Otherwise I'd just have my supper and then this.

Mind you, it is so good that I could never regret it, however tight the dress I might have to wear the next day.

The method is slightly odd, but, again, it's what works for me.

4 slices white bread, cut from a loaf
2 teaspoons mayonnaise
$^1/_2$ teaspoon Worcestershire sauce
75g Cheddar, thinly sliced

1 tomato, thinly sliced
pepper
2 teaspoons olive oil (not extra virgin)

1 Heat a ridged griddle.

2 Get out the bread. Mix the mayonnaise with the Worcestershire sauce and spread on each slice.

3 Now divide the Cheddar and tomato between two slices of bread, grind some pepper over them, and top with the other two slices of bread.

4 Grasping a sandwich in one hand, use the other hand to dip a pastry brush in the oil and then brush the outside of the sandwich with it; proceed in the same way with the second sandwich.

5 Put the sandwiches on the (now hot) griddle and put a frying pan (or another griddle) on top, then add heavy cans of soup or jars of pickles or, amusingly, some exercise weights, and grill pinned down like this for 2 minutes a side.

6 Remove to two waiting plates. Serve with slaw if desired.

Serves 2

SANDWICH SLAW

1 Red Delicious apple, cored and
    chopped into strip-like shapes
1 carrot, cut into matchsticks
75g finely sliced or shredded
    Chinese leaf
$^1/_2$ teaspoon caraway seeds

1 x 15ml tablespoon mango chutney
2 x 15ml tablespoons mayonnaise
1 x 15ml tablespoon lemon juice
$^1/_4$ teaspoon Maldon salt or pinch of
    table salt

1 Put the strips of apple and carrot into a large bowl with the shredded Chinese leaf and toss to mix.

2 In another, small, bowl, mix the caraway seeds with the mango chutney, mayonnaise, lemon juice and salt. Spatula this over the salad in the big bowl, and mix well to combine and coat, before arranging on the plates of sandwiches.

Serves 2

JUMBLEBERRY CRUMBLE

Since you never know when you might be in urgent need of a crumble, I make up enough topping for at least 4 of these and let it sit safely in the freezer until required. Sprinkle it over your fruit of choice as it is, and cook from frozen. Sounds easy, doesn't it?

As for the fruit, I take all chopping out of the equation and give it parity with the crumble topping by using frozen mixed summer fruits; "jumbleberry" is just an old, English term for whatever mixture of berries were used in jams or puddings or jellies.

FOR THE CRUMBLE TOPPING

100g flour

1/2 teaspoon baking powder

50g cold butter, cut into small cubes

3 x 15ml tablespoons Demerara sugar

1 Put the flour and baking powder into a bowl and rub in the cubes of butter, using your fingers until you have a mixture like coarse sand. This is such a small amount, it's not really worth getting out the heavy machinery.

2 Stir in the sugar and then put into a freezer bag to freeze.

This mixture is enough to make 4 jumbleberry crumbles in the cups (as in the photo to the left), and about 8 ramekins

FOR 1 CRUMBLE-IN-A-CUP (approx. 300ml capacity)

100g frozen summer fruits

1 teaspoon cornflour

2 teaspoons vanilla sugar (or regular sugar and drop of vanilla)

75g frozen crumble topping

FOR 1 CRUMBLE-IN-A-RAMEKIN (approx. 125ml capacity)

50g frozen summer fruits

1/2 teaspoon cornflour

1 1/2 teaspoons vanilla sugar (or regular sugar and a drop of vanilla)

30g frozen crumble topping

1 Preheat the oven to 220°C/gas mark 7. Put the summer fruits in either a cup or ramekin and sprinkle the cornflour and sugar over the top. Stir around a little.

2 Sprinkle the frozen crumble topping over the fruit and bake the cup for 20 minutes and the ramekin for 15 minutes.

Serves 1

ROLY POLY PUDDING

I feel better just contemplating this. You get the comfort of a syrup pudding steamed for many, many hours in 30 minutes. And you do practically nothing to make it: roll out half a 375g packet of good shop-bought pastry, ooze golden syrup over it, roll it up like a swiss roll and bung it in a dish, throwing over some milk before putting it in the oven.

You can eat with either cream or ice cream: whatever, it is the perfect Sunday lunch pudding, though there is a good case for making it any day of the week.

1 x 185g slab shop-bought shortcrust pastry, thawed if frozen	240g golden syrup 125ml full-fat milk

1 Preheat the oven to 200°C/gas mark 6. Roll out the pastry to a size about 18 x 32.5cm.

2 Pour the golden syrup onto the pastry, leaving a 2cm margin around the edge.

3 With a buttered oval gratin dish (28cm long) at the ready, roll up the pastry from the short side into a fat sausage shape.

4 Transfer to the dish, putting the seam underneath, and pour half of the milk down one side of the roly-poly and half down the other side.

5 Bake in the oven for 30 minutes.

Serves 4, or 1 under certain stressful conditions

BUTTERFLY CAKES

These were the first cakes I ever made as a child – little fairy cakes with a disc gouged out of their pointy tops (or not, and see evidence to the left), which is then cut in two and the two pieces of cake-top set in a blob of buttercream to look like a pair of butterfly's wings. And, even now, they make me feel strangely comforted. (I say "strangely" as there is nothing comforting about the state of childhood. But then, the false solace gained from lying to yourself about the past is probably a necessary evil.)

But what am I talking about? Just make the cakes. They're very easy to do. I whip cream with food colouring rather than making buttercream, and take comfort from their pretty pastelness.

125g soft butter	1 teaspoon baking powder
125g sugar	1 teaspoon vanilla extract
2 eggs	500ml double cream
125g plain flour	food colouring pastes of your choice
½ teaspoon bicarbonate of soda	(optional)

1 Preheat the oven to 200°C/gas mark 6 and line a 12-bun muffin tin with muffin papers.

2 Cream the butter and sugar either in a bowl by hand or with an electric mixer.

3 Once light and fluffy, add the eggs one at a time with a little of the flour, beating as you go.

4 Fold in the rest of the flour, the bicarbonate of soda, baking powder and, finally, the vanilla.

5 Spoon the batter into the muffin papers, dividing it equally between them.

6 Put in the oven and bake for 15–20 minutes, or until the cupcakes are cooked and golden on top. Take the cupcakes, in their paper cases, out of the tin and let cool on a wire rack.

7 Once they're cool, for each cake, cut off the mounded peak (if your cakes have obliged) or dig out a disk as I did (left), then cut the peak or disc in half to make the butterfly wings. Dig down into each cake a little with your knife. This will leave a small hole to put the cream in to hold the wings. If your cakes haven't peaked much, you will just have to cut a slightly wider circle out of the top, digging in as you do so.

8 Whip the cream until thick, colouring with colour pastes if you wish, and dollop about 2 teaspoonfuls of cream on top of each cake.

9 Stick on your butterfly wings, using the cream as the glue.

Makes 12

Doughnut French Toast

My weaknesses are mainly savoury – think salt and vinegar crisps or cheese and biscuits – but there are times when only a doughnut will do. This craving can get desperate late at night when the shops are shut, and even if they weren't, none of them sells the kind of doughnuts I dream of. This is my way of assuaging my appetite, appeasing my need or, perhaps more accurately, feeding my addiction. Hot chocolate on the side is always worth considering, but just – just! – by itself this is sublime succour.

However, you can, if you like, turn this into a dinner party doughnut-allusive dessert by whizzing up 150g hulled strawberries, 4 tablespoons icing sugar and a spritz of lemon juice in the blender, to make a sauce to pour or puddle over.

2 eggs
4 teaspoons vanilla extract
60ml full-fat milk
4 slices from a small white loaf or
** 2 slices from a large white loaf,**
** each large slice cut in half**

25g butter, plus a drop of flavourless
** oil for frying**
50g caster sugar

1   Beat the eggs with the milk and vanilla in a wide, shallow bowl.

2   Soak the bread halves in the eggy mixture for 5 minutes a side.

3   Heat the butter and oil in a frying pan, and fry the egg-soaked bread until golden and scorched in parts on both sides.

4   Put the sugar on a plate and then dip the cooked bread in it until coated like a sugared doughnut.

Serves 2

TOTALLY CHOCOLATE CHOCOLATE CHIP COOKIES

Along with chocolate, there is much comfort to be gleaned from reading cookbooks. This recipe combines two loves by being chocolatey to the point of madness and having revealed itself to me after a cosy, snuggled-down read of Elinor Klivans' glorious *Big Fat Cookies*. What I do is make up the full batch of these (hard to divide it really, since it contains only 1 egg) and form all 12 cookies, but bake only half and freeze the other half. I freeze them on a little tray and, once they're hard, I bung them in a freezer bag, seal it and stash it back in the freezer, to bake them unthawed at a later date. That way, I've got 6 chocolate cookies to keep me and my family happy without any time or effort.

This is what I call an investment. And it's worth it – these are the chocolatiest cookies you will ever come across.

125g dark chocolate, minimum 70% cocoa solids
150g flour
30g cocoa, sieved
1 teaspoon bicarbonate of soda
$1/2$ teaspoon salt
125g soft butter

75g light brown sugar
50g white sugar
1 teaspoon vanilla extract
1 egg, cold from the fridge
350g (2 bags) semi-sweet chocolate morsels or dark chocolate chips

1 Preheat the oven to 170°C/gas mark 3. Melt the 125g dark chocolate either in the microwave or in a heatproof dish over a pan of simmering water.

2 Put the flour, cocoa, bicarbonate of soda and salt into a bowl.

3 Cream the butter and sugars in another bowl. (I use my freestanding mixer, itself an odd source of comfort to me.) Add the melted chocolate and mix together.

4 Beat in the vanilla extract and cold egg, and then mix in the dry ingredients. Finally stir in the chocolate morsels or chips.

5 Scoop out 12 equal-sized mounds – an ice cream scoop and a palette knife are the best tools for the job – and place on a lined baking sheet about 6cm apart. Do not flatten them.

6 Cook for 18 minutes, testing with a cake tester to make sure it comes out semi-clean and not wet with cake batter. If you pierce a chocolate chip, try again.

7 Leave to cool slightly on the baking sheet for 4–5 minutes, then transfer them to a cooling rack to harden as they cool.

Makes 12

Razzle Dazzle

ometimes you have people over for supper; sometimes you have a party. And the trouble is, just because you've planned on giving this party, doesn't mean you have the time to prepare for it. Count yourself lucky. I know that I have perhaps an overdeveloped antipathy to the formal and fancy, but I do think that not having very much time to prepare means you are less likely to go over the top and more likely to throw a party that you and your guests will enjoy.

The problem with those incredibly detailed, perfectionist-pleasing party plans is that they can reduce the guests to mere cogs in the machine. You're not worried about whether they're having a good time, just whether everything's going according to plan. Sound familiar?

I have nothing against getting out the best china and making the table look beautiful, though I'm rather of the opinion that any table groaning with food is beautiful, crockery be damned. As for a party that involves standing up and picking at things, rather than sitting down and feasting on them, then I agree that all effort must be made. But this doesn't mean you have to take two days off work to make the place look the part. I'm all for easy, simple touches. I drape all available surfaces – bookshelves, mantelpieces, side tables – with grapes and assorted fruits, aiming on the whole to evoke the bounty of a Roman bacchanalia; I want the guests to be surrounded by fruitful plenty, as if welcoming sumptuousness were just spilling out of every corner.

Flowers, I think, should be present but modest: don't go in for flashy, expensive displays but rather choose a panoply of smaller flowers that will fit in smaller vases. And although I say vases, I mean little bottles, canisters, beakers and any receptacle that inspires. A case in point: I like to use those small glass pots that fancy French yoghurts come in; and, eccentric as it sounds, empty cans – of Italian tomatoes, olives, chestnuts, golden syrup, exotic foreign ingredients, especially when the writing on the cans is in a different script – make fabulous vases, especially in profusion. And I am forever buying odd little jars and containers from eBay to dot about the place with a sprig or two of something beautiful. Remember, it doesn't have to be flowers: think parsley, rosemary, mint and any other foliage you can get your hands on. But, whatever you use, just bear in mind that what works best is to have as many little pots as possible scattered about the place. I rather like going about the house strewing it with fruits and flowers and anything beauteous. It gets me in party mood.

You need to be practical, too, so remember plates for detritus, ashtrays – sorry to offend the anti-tobacco lobby – stacks of napkins (paper is fine). My mother could never resist finger bowls either, and there is something to be said for filling small dishes with warm water and a slice of lemon, and drop of rosewater too if you're exotically inclined. On the whole, though, people tend not to use them these days, so your thoughtfulness may be wasted and you may be casting pearls before swine, if that's not too rude a way to talk about your friends.

Kingsley Amis once said that the three most depressing words in the English language were "red or white?" and I think of this every time I throw a party. It was whisky he wanted to drink, but I don't think you need supply spirits, just add some other drink that seems to strike a party note. If it's a relatively restrained assembly, in terms of numbers, this is what I like to do: get lots of dry fizzy wine and make sure it is really properly chilled and then lay out a display of flavoured syrups, the sort barmen keep behind their bar, and you can pour everyone their wine and let them experiment with the syrup of their choice. My Monin syrups (bought, conveniently, online from www.thedrinkshop.com along with any recherché liqueur I ever need) are beginning to look like some technicolour army advancing across my kitchen; favourites (with my friends) to splosh into the sparkling wine are Rose, Watermelon, Pomegranate and Passionfruit. I bring out a different range for Christmas parties (think Cranberry, Winter Berry, Toffee Nut and Gingerbread, and see pages 316 and 318) and, curious I know, I love these in beer, too. Speaking of which, if you're serving beer as well at your party, which I think you should if it's summer or if dancing is involved, you must make sure it's so cold it hurts.

As for the food, I never think you should make masses of different things. I go for a choice of three, but those three in abundance. Though whatever bits and pieces you do offer people to eat, it's always worth baking trays of cocktail sausages in addition. I would feel I weren't giving a proper party without sausages. Putting sausages in the oven and then taking them out again, scarcely counts as work either. If you want to make things easier still, use throwaway foil roasting trays. I have nothing against dotting the room with bought snacky things. You don't have to be embarrassed about serving those rather compelling Japanese rice crackers so long as you're providing real food, too. My absolute favourite are the wasabi-coated peas you can sometimes find in specialist stores, but they do blow your head off, so perhaps they're not for everyone.

Sit-down dinners, when you are filled with the desire to do something special but haven't got the time to back it up, needn't pose a problem. Again, I believe that anything that stops you boning partridges or spinning sugar can only be good. I keep the food simple, but the mood sumptuous. My idea of razzle dazzle is not that you are needily trying to impress everyone, but rather you are conjuring up an evening that wows with the least amount of work possible.

A final note on the hardest part of any even semi-formal dinner, the *placement*. I hate, hate, hate drawing up seating plans. If you have one, then people become anxious about their position in the pecking order; if you don't, they all hover about nervously not sitting down or knowing what to do, and you are obliged to produce an instant *placement* out of your head. So it's a disaster either way.

This is my way through it all. I number each place and then I fill a hat with another pile of numbers (either buy books of raffle tickets or make your own) and I get people to take a number on their way in. This way they know where to sit but don't feel sensitive about their position. If you like to keep things girl-boy-girl-boy – which never worries me, I must say – then just do, as it were, a pink set of numbers and a blue set of numbers and two hats or receptacles by the door. There needs to be a system, even if that system is random. Such is life.

Green Apple Martini

This is a cocktail with a kick and addictively delicious. I have to say it is enormously useful as a quick shot of party spirit before you go to someone else's party. I always feel better the next day, having a stiff drink before and water (sparkling rather than still but, hey, let's live a little) during a party.

Although it is a sour apple Martini, at home I refer to it only as Kryptonite. The lurid green is quite something.

I've given quantities per glass simply because it's better made up glass by glass and you can hand them round to your guests as they request them. I wouldn't want to make these for a huge roomful of people, but they are perfect as a way of helping those who've hot-footed from the office, weary from the working day, unwind at the beginning of a dinner party. If you want huge jugfuls to pass round, either go for the White Lady on page 57 or the red Ginger Pom below.

1 shot vodka or gin
1 shot sour apple liqueur

$^1/_2$ shot Monin Green Apple syrup
1 slice Granny Smith apple

1   In a martini glass, combine the vodka or gin over lots of ice, and add the apple liqueur and the green apple syrup.

2   Slice a segment of apple, removing any core. Cut a nick horizontally in the bottom of the slice, and slip it onto the edge of the glass.

Serves 1 – and how!

Ginger Pom

This drink started off as my non-alcoholic alternative for teetotallers (obviously without the liqueur) and I still make it like that. But then I came across some pomegranate liqueur and knew it had a place here. By all means have two jugs, one with the boozy version, one with just juice and dry ginger, but make sure you and other people can easily distinguish between the two by putting, say, lime slices in the alcohol-free jug. And in either case, make sure this is good and cold.

1 part Pama pomegranate liqueur
2 parts pomegranate juice

2 parts ginger ale
ice cubes

1   What can I say? Mix these ingredients together and pour over ice.

Serves 1

POTATO CAKES WITH SMOKED SALMON

I've done many versions of potato pancakes, in my life, but this has got to be the easiest. I shocked myself by making it with Smash (instant mash), but there has to be a first time. And they taste wonderful, so no need to feel bad. But if having an ingredient like this in your storecupboard makes you feel too trailer-trash for words, then go to some expensive healthstore and buy a packet of organic potato flakes instead. I do understand.

I have to tell you that if you make these with 100g instant mashed potato granules and no flour or baking powder, you have the most stodgily fabulous squat little cakes to eat with a proper fried breakfast. These are mighty good for soaking up excess, if delicious, fats and juices, but a more elegant version is required here. Hand them round at cocktail parties or lay out the component parts on the table for an appetizer, adding a little bowl of crème fraîche, sour cream or *smetana*.

FOR THE POTATO CAKES

3 eggs
125ml full-fat milk
2 spring onions, finely sliced
2 x 15ml tablespoons olive oil
60g instant mashed potato granules

40g flour
$^1/_2$ teaspoon baking powder
$^1/_2$ teaspoon lemon juice

FOR THE TOPPING

300g smoked salmon

1 small bunch or packet fresh dill

1 In a batter jug, whisk the eggs, milk, finely sliced spring onions and olive oil together.

2 Stir in the potato granules, flour and baking powder and, finally, the lemon juice.

3 Heat a flat griddle, and drop 15ml-tablespoonfuls of the mixture onto the hot griddle.

4 Cook for about 30 seconds a side, or until golden brown and firm enough at the sides to flip.

5 Once you have made the pancakes, and they've cooled a little, tear off tiny strips of smoked salmon and arrange the small slices on each pancake.

6 Decorate each salmon-topped pancake with a tiny feather of dill.

Makes 30

THE INSTANT CANAPÉ: QUICK CROSTINI WITH AVOCADO AND GREEN PEA HUMMUS

I love avocados and I've already confessed my *faiblesse* for processed peas, so it stands to reason that one day I was going to try them together. It doesn't sound altogether modest to say this, but it is a triumph. I cannot tell you how quickly these disappear.

Not only is the avocado and green pea hummus a doddle to make, but just to add to your ease, I suggest you use a packet of pumpernickel rounds as the crostini-base. If you can't get hold of them, just buy a French stick or a *ficelle* and slice and so on, as on page 239. But the party-pumpernickel should be your first choice.

By all means use the green-green hummus as a dip if you want, though you'll need lots (add a spoon or two of Philadelphia when mixing too) and serve surrounded with sugar-snaps, sliced sweet peppers and other crudités of your choice.

It should go without saying that you can replace the canned peas with frozen peas – or indeed fresh – which you cook, purée and cool before mixing with the avocado. Lovely but less express.

1 ripe avocado
2 x 15ml tablespoons lime juice
$^1/_2$ clove garlic, crushed
1 teaspoon Maldon salt or
   $^1/_2$ teaspoon table salt

1 x 300g can marrow fat peas, drained
1 x 250g packet (30) cocktail
   pumpernickel rounds (or 8 regular
   pumpernickel slices, each cut into
   4 little squares)

1 Spoon out the flesh of the avocado into a food processor, and add the lime juice and crushed garlic.

2 Add the salt and drained peas and then process until you have a Kermit-coloured purée.

3 Spread the pumpernickel rounds softly with the avocado and pea mixture and arrange on a large platter for serving.

Makes 30

RAZZLE DAZZLE

TUNA AND CRAB & AVOCADO WRAPS

I have never really thought of myself as a person who could wrap, fold or fiddle about with food or felt that way inclined. But you know, when you get into it, it's really quite OK – actually, more than OK. These wraps are curiously relaxing to assemble and everyone is always bowled over by them. They're a very good way of injecting a little zing into the proceedings without having to slave for hours over a hot hob.

I have added the option of the crab wraps as I do understand not everyone is happy working with or even eating raw tuna. But please try those, too: they are actually a very unspooky experience. Just be sure to ask a fishmonger for sashimi-grade tuna and buy it the day you want to eat it.

For both these recipes I've given the basic unit of wrap; that's to say, amounts are sufficient to fill 1 tortilla, which in turn will yield 3 pieces once rolled and cut.

FOR THE TUNA WRAPS

1 teaspoon mayonnaise

$1/2$ teaspoon wasabi paste

1–2 drops sesame oil

1 soft flour tortilla wrap

$1/2$ carrot, peeled and cut into matchsticks

$1/4$ cucumber, halved lengthways, deseeded and cut into matchsticks

1 x 75g tuna, sliced into 3mm x 2cm rectangles

1 Whisk together the mayonnaise, wasabi and sesame oil in a small bowl, and paint the tortilla wrap with this mixture on one side.

2 Arrange a row of carrot sticks horizontally 2–3cm up from the bottom of the wrap in front of you.

3 Arrange the cucumber on top of the carrot in the same way, or as best as you can – it may slip down a little.

4 Top with the slices of tuna, also laid horizontally as this makes it easy to wrap up.

5 Roll up the wrap as tightly as you can, starting from the bottom. You want to end up with a shape resembling a fat Cuban cigar.

6 Cut across the rolled wrap diagonally to make 3 pieces.

FOR THE CRAB AND AVOCADO WRAPS

70g white crab meat

1 teaspoon mayonnaise

$1/2$ teaspoon wasabi paste

1–2 drops sesame oil

$1/2$ avocado

4 x 15ml tablespoons finely shredded iceberg lettuce

squeeze of lemon juice

1 soft flour tortilla wrap

1   Put the crab meat into a bowl, add the mayonnaise, wasabi paste and oil, and stir to mix.

2   Lay the wrap in front of you and put the crab meat in a horizontal line 2–3cm up from the bottom of the wrap.

3   Take the avocado half, still with skin on, and scoop out the flesh in half-teaspoonful curls, laying these on top of the line of crab meat.

4   Sprinkle the lettuce in a neat line on top of the avocado, and then spritz with the lemon juice.

5   Roll up tightly from the bottom, to form a fat cigar shape and then slice on an angle into three.

The two recipes combined make 6 pieces

Juicy Beef Skewers with Horseradish Dip

This is another recipe that you can bring into play for people who are standing up and milling around, or as a first course for a sit-down meal.

I find fresh horseradish easy to come by these days but, if you don't, add the same amount of hot horseradish cream or sauce from a jar for the marinade.

If you want to serve lamb skewers alongside, then use cubed leg, replace the horseradish in the marinade with a teaspoonful each of ground cumin and coriander, and make a dip by mixing good shop-bought hummus with Greek-style plain yogurt, and drizzle the top with a little olive oil before scattering with some pomegranate seeds.

500g beef rump
$1^1/_2$ x 15ml tablespoons of good-quality red wine vinegar or balsamic vinegar
3 x 15ml tablespoons freshly grated horseradish or hot horseradish sauce or cream
2 x 15ml tablespoons rosemary needles (or 1 teaspoon dried rosemary), plus 1 bunch rosemary for garnish (optional)

60ml olive oil
2 x 15ml tablespoons Worcestershire sauce
2 x 15ml tablespoons port
200g crème fraîche or sour cream
$^1/_2$ teaspoon Dijon mustard
$^1/_4$ teaspoon Maldon salt or generous pinch of table salt
4 x 15ml tablespoons chopped chives

1 Cut the beef into 2.5cm cubes, and put into a freezer bag with the vinegar and 1 tablespoon of the freshly grated horseradish or 1 tablespoon hot horseradish sauce. Add the 2 tablespoons of fresh rosemary (or 1 teaspoon of dried), and the olive oil, Worcestershire sauce and port. Leave for at least 20 minutes, but preferably overnight, in the fridge.

2 Let the meat come to room temperature, and soak about 10 bamboo skewers in water at the same time.

3 Make the dip, by beating together the crème fraîche or sour cream, the remaining 2 tablespoons of freshly grated horseradish or 2 tablespoons hot horseradish sauce, the Dijon mustard, salt and the chives, leaving some chives to sprinkle over the top.

4 Heat a grill or griddle, then thread 3 or 4 pieces of meat onto each skewer and slap on the heat, turning after 2 minutes. Cook for another 2 minutes on the other side and then remove to a plate, strewn with some sprigs of rosemary if desired. Do not serve while grill-hot.

Makes approx. 10 skewers

Red-Leaf, Fig and Serrano Ham Salad

This salad takes mere minutes to make, and yet is enduringly beautiful. I don't overstate the case; there is something positively painterly about the delicate heaping of dark red leaves, red-bellied figs, and deep pink ham. I love the sharpness of Manchego, dropped in feathery shavings among all this, but don't panic if the cheese eludes you (though my supermarket does stock it). Just use some Parmesan or pecorino instead.

1 head treviso or radicchio
200g baby ruby chard or 2 bags salad
   with red-toned tender leaves
2 teaspoons sherry vinegar
2 x 15ml tablespoons extra virgin
   olive oil

pinch of salt
8 fresh figs, quartered
275g Serrano ham slices, cut very
   thinly
50g Manchego cheese

1   Tear the head of treviso or radicchio into manageable pieces, and toss together with the baby salad leaves.

2   Whisk together the vinegar, oil and salt in a small bowl and then dress the leaves.

3   Arrange the figs and ham with as much artistry as you can muster over the salad and then, with a potato peeler, shave the cheese over, letting it fall lightly where it will.

Serves 8

Scallops-on-the-Shell

I can't quite believe how simple yet luscious these are. I prefer to get my scallops from the fishmonger for this, which is just as well as I don't think I could ever get a supermarket to supply me with shells.

You don't need to take the corals off, but I like to turn this into two meals, and fry up the corals the next day, with some butter and garlic oil and eat them squished onto chunky bread or toast, and spritzed with lemon juice and carpeted with parsley.

These are really a starter, but I certainly wouldn't mind knocking a couple of shells' worth back for a special supper any day of the week.

6 scallop shells	6 teaspoons butter
18 scallops (or 24 if very small), roes or corals removed	1 lime, cut for squeezing
	$1^1/_2$ teaspoons garlic oil
100g fresh breadcrumbs	salt and pepper to taste

1 Preheat the oven to 250°C/gas mark 9 (you need a really hot oven). Rinse and dry the scallop shells and arrange them on a baking sheet.

2 Put the scallops in a bowl and sprinkle the breadcrumbs over them. Toss them around to get each one well coated in crumbs.

3 Put 3 breaded scallops into each shell and sprinkle with any leftover breadcrumbs that remain in the bottom of the bowl.

4 Add 1 teaspoon of butter on top of each scallop-filled shell, a squirt of lime juice, $^1/_4$ teaspoon of garlic oil, and salt and pepper to taste.

5 Put the scallops in the oven for about 15–20 minutes – you really want the breadcrumbs to be crispy and the butter turning black around the edges of the shell.

Serves 6

Duck Breasts with Pomegranate and Mint

This is my idea of perfect dinner party food: it's easy to make, not complicated to serve and looks – and tastes – exquisite.

Feel free to griddle or grill your duck, rather than just sear it on the hob and then roast it, but I find I make the air too smoky when it's all done on the hob.

I advise asking a friend into the kitchen to help you slice the meat. Obviously, it's not exactly hard work carving a duck breast, but so that the first slices aren't cold by the time the last ones go on the serving platter, it makes sense to speed up the process. This is not crucial: it doesn't really matter what temperature these jewelled slivers of meat are.

4 duck breasts
200g rocket, watercress or salad chard (or a mixture)
1 pomegranate
1 small bunch or packet mint

1 Preheat the oven to 220°C/gas mark 7.

2 Heat a flameproof, ovenproof pan on the hob, and then sear the duck breasts, skin-side down, for a minute or so over a high heat.

3 Turn the duck breasts over and then place in the oven for about 15 minutes.

4 Remove the duck breasts from the oven and sit them on a carving board while you get organized. If you want to hold them at this stage, take them out of the oven at about 13 minutes and double-wrap in foil, then let them sit till you need them.

5 Line a meat plate or flattish platter with the salad leaves.

6 Slice each duck breast very thinly on the diagonal and lay on the salad-lined dish, pouring any meat juices over them as you go.

7 Halve the pomegranate, and then bash out the seeds from one half to garnish the duck slices. Squeeze some of the juice from the other half – just by hand – over the duck as well.

8 Tear off a handful of mint leaves and then finely chop them, scattering them over the duck.

Serves 8

GRIDDLED VENISON WITH PINK GIN APPLE SAUCE AND ROAST PENCIL LEEKS

There is a certain mellow elegance to this dinner, despite the scant demands it places on you, the cook. I am happy to griddle rather than roast the venison, since the leanness of the meat means you don't get much smoke, but if you're happier stashing it in the oven, be my guest.

I like to serve this with some pickled red cabbage alongside; its piquancy is the perfect counterfoil to the sweet dense flesh. I don't want anything else, not if I plan to make serious headway into any of the puddings which follow. Nevertheless, consider a good lazy side dish; some really good-quality plain potato crisps warmed in the oven are the kind of accompaniment no one, however carb-fearing, can manage to resist.

750g venison loin	2 teaspoons black peppercorns
125ml gin	1 onion, quartered
2 teaspoons Worcestershire sauce	2 star anise
60ml olive oil	2 garlic cloves, bruised

1 Put the venison into a large freezer bag and add the remaining ingredients. Leave out for at least 20 minutes, or if you can afford the time up to 2 hours, or even overnight in the fridge.

2 When you are ready to cook the meat, heat a large griddle until almost smoking hot.

3 Take the venison out of the marinade (discard the marinade), shaking it well, then slap down onto the hot griddle and cook for about 15 minutes, turning frequently to gain even scorch marks. When the venison is ready, remove to a carving board to rest, loosely tented with foil, before slicing thinly.

Serves 6

PINK GIN APPLE SAUCE

Don't just buy bottled apple sauce; it's this that makes the venison special. If you own a food mill (and they are not expensive to buy), it's risibly easy to make.

5 spring onions (white part only), finely sliced	2 x 15ml tablespoons gin, plus 1 teaspoon
2 x 15ml tablespoons butter	juice of 1 lemon
sprinkling of salt	1 long red chilli, left whole
3 Red Delicious apples	

1. In a wide saucepan with a lid, soften the white shreds of spring onion in the butter, adding a little salt to prevent it scorching.

2. Cut the apples in half, and then each half into quarters (without bothering to core) and add to the pan with the onion. Pour in the 2 tablespoons of gin, the lemon juice and whole chilli, giving everything a good stir.

3. Cover the pan and cook at a medium heat until the apples are soft (this should take no more than 20 minutes).

4. Take out the chilli pepper, and then work the sauce through a food mill or sieve, the skins from the apples colouring the sauce a blushing dusky pink. Stir in the remaining teaspoon of gin and season to taste.

5. Serve the pink gin apple sauce with the venison either in a separate bowl or at one side of the plate of venison.

Serves 6 as an accompaniment

ROAST PENCIL LEEKS

I love this as a vegetable accompaniment but I should tell you it also works very well, at room temperature, with some dressing over it, as a starter. If you can't find the baby leeks – though there seems to an alarming proliferation of baby vegetables these days – then simply substitute some fat spring onions.

> 300g miniature leeks
> 3 x 15ml tablespoons garlic oil
> 1 teaspoon Maldon salt or $^1/_2$ teaspoon table salt
> juice of $^1/_2$ lemon

1. Preheat the oven to 220°C/gas mark 7.

2. Lay the leeks in a large, shallow baking dish or roasting tin and add the oil and salt, then roll the leeks about to coat well.

3. Cook in the blistering oven for about 15 minutes, by which time they should be bronzed in parts.

4. Decant to a serving dish, and spritz with the lemon juice.

Serves 6

TARTE FINE AUX POMMES

This is the chic version of my lumpy-bumpy galette on page 156. I normally find something fascistically threatening about symmetry, but the lined-up orderliness of this is too beautiful to abhor. Plus, it tastes fantastic and is easy-peasy to make. What more do you want?

2 large Granny Smith apples (or 3 smaller ones)
juice of 1 lemon
1 x approx. 375g sheet (40 x 23cm) all-butter shop-bought ready-rolled puff pastry, defrosted if frozen

2 x 15ml tablespoons of sugar
1 x 15ml tablespoon butter
crème fraîche for serving if wished

1 Preheat the oven to 220°C/gas mark 7.

2 Core the apples, and cut them in half. Pour the lemon juice into a wide, shallow dish and top up with some cold water. Immerse the apple halves in the lemony water; this will stop them turning brown.

3 Lay the sheet of puff pastry on a large lined baking sheet, and, using either the back of a large carving knife or a steel ruler, mark a 1cm border all the way round the edge of the rectangle. You need to score the lines on the pastry rather than cutting all the way through it. This will allow a frame to rise above the apple filling.

4 Take the apple halves out of the lemony water and pat dry. Cut each half into quarters, then slice each quarter as thinly as you possibly can: think segment wafers.

5 Sprinkle 1 tablespoon of sugar over the base. Working from the inside edge, place the apple slices, closely overlapping, within the border of the frame. Create neat lines of apple slices until the pastry is covered.

6 Heat the butter with the remaining tablespoon of sugar in a small pan, and let both bubble for a few minutes until a light caramel colour appears. Dribble this syrup over the apples and put the tart in the oven.

7 Bake for 20–25 minutes, by which time a puff pastry border will have risen around the apples, and the fruit will be soft and slightly coloured. Cut into squares or slices.

Serves 6–8

White Chocolate Mint Mousse

I am not normally much of a white chocolate person, but the peppermint in this recipe seems to eradicate its lethal richness. Nevertheless, my nephew did say of it, when I let him have some for a birthday treat, that it was like being able to eat the icing without having the cake. He wasn't speaking figuratively. And because it is rich and sweet, I serve it in uncharacteristically small portions. As they say in showbiz, always good to leave 'em wanting more.

250g white chocolate, broken into small pieces
250ml double cream
1 egg white

$^1/_4$ teaspoon peppermint extract (I use Boyajian Natural Peppermint Flavour)
6 fresh mint leaves (optional)

1 Put the pieces of white chocolate in a heatproof bowl, and sit this bowl over a pan of simmering water until the chocolate melts, stirring gently with a spatula every now and then. When it's melted, stand the bowl on a cold surface to cool down a little.

2 In another bowl, and using an electric handheld whisk for ease, whip the cream, egg white and peppermint together. You want a softly peaking rather than stiff mixture.

3 Put a big dollop of cream onto the slightly cooled chocolate and mix in, and then gently fold this chocolate mixture into the cream.

4 Divide the mixture between six small but perfectly formed glasses – like the ones opposite – with a capacity of 6oml each.

5 Chill in the fridge or give them a fast icy zap by sitting them in the deep freeze for 10 or 15 minutes. Decorate each glass with a mint leaf (if using) on serving.

Serves 6

GLITZY CHOCOLATE PUDDINGS

If you've got an electric whisk – either a hand one or a freestanding mixer – this is very low effort indeed, but it is a real showstopper. There's something quite extraordinary about the greedy silence that falls over the table as you put these out.

The glitz is provided by their utter fantabulousness and the scattering of honeycomb over the top. If you don't want to use a Crunchie bar, of course buy some honeycomb or make Hokey Pokey (see page 281), or else scatter with finely chopped pistachios. You will lose the sugary-glitter look, but you will still have brought to life an elegantly voluptuous creation.

100g dark chocolate, minimum 70% cocoa solids
100g soft butter
200g sugar
4 eggs
50g flour
1/4 teaspoon bicarbonate of soda
pinch of salt

FOR THE GLAZE
150g dark chocolate, minimum 70% cocoa solids
45g butter
2 x 40g Crunchie bars, broken into shards

1 Preheat the oven to 180°C/gas mark 4.

2 Break up the chocolate and melt it with the butter in a bowl in the microwave or in a double boiler. Once it's melted, sit the bowl on a cold surface so that the chocolate cools.

3 Preferably in a freestanding mixer, beat the eggs and sugar until thick and pale and moussy, then gently fold in the flour, bicarbonate of soda and a pinch of salt.

4 Fold in the slightly cooled chocolate and butter mixture and then divide between eight ramekins, put in the oven to bake for 25 minutes.

5 Meanwhile, get on with the glaze by melting the chocolate and butter in a microwave (or double boiler), then whisk to form a smooth glossy mixture, and spoon this over the cooked puddings.

6 Decorate with Crunchie rubble: I just put the bars in a freezer bag, set to with a rolling pin and strew over the top.

Serves 8

ICE CREAM CAKE

I don't think a cook's job should be to deceive, but there is something appealing about the fact that this looks and tastes as if it were incredibly hard work and yet involves no more than a bit of stirring. You must, though, serve a warm sauce with it – the crowning glory – and I've certainly given you options below.

To be frank, you can choose different biscuits, different nuts and nobbly bits to mix in with the ice cream and give crunch, texture and sudden shards of flavour. I find it hard to believe, however, that this could be in any way improved. Sorry, but that's just how it is.

1.5 litres ice cream
100g honey roast peanuts
200g Nestlé swirled milk chocolate and peanut butter morsels (or chocolate chips of your choice)
1 x 40g Crunchie bar, broken into shards and dusty rubble

150g Bourbon biscuits broken up into crumbs and rubble
1 batch Butterscotch Sauce (see page 27) plus 1 batch Hot Chocolate Sauce (see page 51) or 1 batch Chocolate Peanut Butter Flavour Sauce (see page 160)

1 Let the ice cream soften either in the fridge for a while, or out in the kitchen.

2 Line a 20cm springform tin with clingfilm, both in the bottom and sides of the tin so that you have some overhang at the top.

3 Empty the slightly softened ice cream into a bowl and mix in the peanuts, 150g chocolate and peanut butter morsels or chocolate chips, Crunchie shards and 100g of the Bourbon biscuit crumbs.

4 Scrape the ice cream mixture into the springform tin, flattening the top like a cake, cover the top with clingfilm and place in the freezer to firm up.

5 Serve the cake straight from the freezer, unmoulding from the tin and pulling the clingfilm gently away, before putting on a plate or cake stand. Let it stand and soften for about 5 minutes before cutting.

6 Sprinkle the top of the cake with the extra 50g of chocolate and peanut butter morsels or chocolate chips, and the remaining Bourbon biscuit crumbs.

7 Cut into slices and serve with the butterscotch and chocolate sauces, letting both dribble lacily over each slice. If two sauces sound like too much trouble – they're not – just opt for the chocolate peanut butter sauce. It's hard to find an argument against it.

Serves 8–10

BLACKBERRIES IN MUSCAT JELLY

This is unlike anything else: the texture is soft set, so you know it's not a liquid but it doesn't have the heft of a solid. And the acidity of the blackberries within the musky sweetness of the jelly is a further thrill.

What I do is to make this in the morning of the evening I want to eat it. It is so straightforward that you can do it groggily at breakfast, no trouble. It doesn't need so long to set, but I find it easier to work like this.

250g blackberries

5 leaves gelatine

625ml Beaumes-de-Venise or other
muscat wine

125ml water

2 x 15ml tablespoons lime juice

100g vanilla or caster sugar

double cream to serve

1 Divide the blackberries between 6 glasses; I use old-fashioned champagne saucers with a capacity of about 200ml each.

2 Soak the gelatine leaves in a dish of cold water for 5 minutes.

3 Put the wine, water, sugar and lime juice in a saucepan over a lowish heat and stir to dissolve the sugar. Bring to the boil and boil for 1 minute before removing the pan from the heat.

4 Wring out the gelatine leaves and place in a cup. Whisk around 100ml of the hot liquid into the gelatine leaves in their cup before pouring the gelatine and liquid mixture into the pan of hot liquid, and whisking well to mix. Allow to cool a little.

5 Pour the liquid over the blackberries in their glasses and refrigerate until set: 3–4 hours depending on how cold your fridge is, or overnight.

6 Serve with some cream in a jug, separately.

Serves 6

GINGER PASSIONFRUIT TRIFLE

I don't think I've ever written a book without a trifle in it, and I'm not about to start now. Besides, this is one of those puddings that looks spectacular, but requires the least amount of effort and scarcely any time at all to make. And by the way, when I say "make", I really mean assemble.

The taste, though, is glorious and, for all its simplicity of construction, it feels like a big deal. Rich, though, which means you can feed a large tableful of people with one fabulous mound.

400–500g shop-bought sponge
   cake, usually 2 loaves (or same
   weight of baker's madeleines)
125ml Stone's Original Green Ginger
   Wine

500ml double cream
4 teaspoons icing sugar
8 passionfruit

1 Slice or break the sponge into pieces and arrange half of them in a shallow dish or cake stand with slight lip or upward curve at edge, then pour half the ginger wine over them. Mound up the remaining half of sponge and pour the remaining ginger wine on top.

2 Whip the cream with the icing sugar until it is firm but not stiff; you want soft peaks.

3 Scoop the insides of 2 passionfruit into the bowl of cream and fold in before mounding the cream floppily over the soused sponge.

4 Scoop out the remaining 6 passionfruit onto the white pile of cream so that it is doused and dribbling with the black seeds and fragrant golden pulp.

Serves 8–10

Speedy
GONZALES

This is embarrassing, but I must get it off my chest before we go any further. I am not remotely qualified to tell anyone anything about Mexican food. I haven't, I regret to say, even been to Mexico.

So, if it would be misleading to claim this as my Mexican chapter, it is truthful to say it's definitely inspired by Mexican food and culture. Let me just add that I don't actually think that avocados and tortillas are all they eat in Mexico, but somehow they seem to be exuberantly represented here. I have always been someone to keep a regular stash of avocados in the house, but now packets of soft tortillas are as much of a staple. If there ain't the wherewithal for a quesadilla in my household, believe me, I'm not allowed to forget it.

If I don't claim authenticity, I can at least say that I have endeavoured not to be crassly inauthentic. No Mexicans have been harmed in the writing of this chapter. To expand: wherever possible I have roped in Mexican friends, or friends of friends, to taste, criticize and act as guinea pigs and their gratifyingly greedy approval has meant a lot to me.

And while it's true that my delight in the chapter's title might have encouraged me initially, the fact of the matter is, my researches, and the food they inspired, have led to some of my favourite recipes in this book. This is not about the lure of the new. I am enough of a traditionalist – in the kitchen at any rate – to be wary of novelty and comforted by the familiar. But this is fast food that is fresh and vibrant, and eating it, in turn, makes you feel more awake and alive.

Mexican Scrambled Eggs

This is not only the best way to start the day, but the best way to end it, too. You can make it even more of a meal by serving some refried beans alongside, but I love it just as it is. It also happens to be one of the greatest hangover cures around. You know, I'm tempted to consider overdoing it partywise just to have an excuse to whip up a batch of these. But then, they are so good that there is always a reason to eat them; no need to scout around for excuses.

2 x 15ml tablespoons vegetable oil
2 soft corn tortillas
1 tomato, deseeded and roughly
    chopped
1 spring onion, roughly chopped

1 small green chilli, deseeded and
    chopped
4 eggs, beaten
$1/4$ teaspoon of Maldon salt or pinch
    of table salt

1 Heat the vegetable oil in a heavy-based frying pan. Roll up the corn tortillas in a sausage shape and then snip them into strips with a pair of scissors straight into the hot oil.

2 Fry the tortilla strips for a few minutes until crisp and golden, and then remove to a bowl.

3 Add the chopped tomato and spring onion to the hot oily pan along with the chopped chilli, turning everything about for a minute or so with a wooden spoon.

4 Put the corn tortilla strips back in the pan, and add the beaten eggs and salt. Using the same spoon, move everything about the pan as you do when scrambling eggs.

5 Once the eggs are setting, remove the pan from the heat, and continue stirring the eggs until they are done to your liking.

Serves 2

Mexican Chicken Salad with Tomato and Black Bean Salsa

This is a lunch fit for the gods, and a pretty divine dinner, outside on a balmy night, too.

A jicama is sometimes known as a Mexican potato, though that's a bit misleading since you can eat it raw. It looks like a turnip wrapped in fresh ginger skin. If you can't get hold of a jicama, then I'd replace it with an Asian or Nashi pear or a couple of drained cans of water chestnuts, cut into matchsticks; what you want is juiciness and crunch. I wouldn't say no to a Granny Smith apple, cut into chunky matchsticks, either.

I admit I had never even heard of a jicama before researching this recipe, but I phoned my greengrocer and he said they were available at market and just to give him some warning. I don't imagine that you can talk a supermarket into stocking them if they don't already have a leaning towards Latin American produce – though you never know – but I like going to small, specialist stores when I can, and this is another good reason why.

The dressing is addictive. I sometimes keep a jar of it in the fridge for a day or two; the lime seems to stave off any browning or blackening of the avocado flesh.

FOR THE DRESSING
1 ripe avocado
125ml sour cream
3 x 15ml tablespoons lime juice
1 garlic clove, peeled
1 teaspoon Maldon salt or $^1/_2$ teaspoon table salt
good grinding of black pepper

FOR THE SALAD
300g shredded cooked chicken
1 x jicama approx. 500g, peeled and cut into 5mm matchsticks, or see alternatives in intro (left)
2 spring onions, finely shredded
cupped handful of finely chopped fresh coriander
125g shredded cos lettuce

1 Spoon the flesh out of the avocado, and put into a blender with all the other dressing ingredients.

2 Process the dressing until smooth.

3 Put all the salad ingredients into a bowl, and spoon the dressing over them, making sure everything gets coated well.

Serves 4–6

Tomato and Black Bean Salsa

I keep jars of green (milder) and red (hotter) jalapeño chilli peppers, and prefer the fieriness of the red here, but it's entirely up to you. And if you'd prefer to use fresh jalapeños, then do.

1 x 425g can black beans
2 tomatoes, deseeded and roughly chopped
1 teaspoon Maldon salt or $^1/_2$ teaspoon table salt

75g roughly chopped pickled red jalapeño chilli peppers from a jar
1 x 15ml tablespoon lime juice

1 Drain and rinse the beans, and then mix in a bowl with the chopped tomatoes, salt, jalapeños and lime juice.

2 Check the seasoning and then serve with the Mexican Chicken Salad, either in a bowl to the side or dolloped on the same plate.

Serves 4–6 as part of this meal

Sweetcorn Chowder with Toasted Tortillas

The tortillas we use here are those crisp, crunchy, corn-gritty triangles that somehow always feel like a guilty pleasure. Although having said that, I know only that "guilty pleasures" exist, but I have never understood the point of feeling guilty about pleasure. Rather, I see plenty of reasons for feeling guilty about failing to take pleasure in things.

When I plan to make this, I tend to take a big pack of frozen corn out of the deep freeze at breakfast time, in readiness for a super-quick, fantastically soothing, mellow-yellow and very pleasing supper that night.

Use whatever cheese you like; mostly I go for Cheddar since I always have some in the fridge, but I am happy about using up other bits and pieces. If children are eating, it's wise to omit the chillis – unless they're being *very* annoying.

1kg frozen sweetcorn, defrosted
3 spring onions, each one debearded
　　and halved
1 clove garlic, peeled
35g semolina
1.5 litres hot vegetable stock made
　　from concentrate or cube

400g lightly salted tortilla chips
200g grated cheese
2 long red chillies, deseeded and
　　finely chopped (optional)

1　Preheat the oven to 200°C/gas mark 6.

2　Drain the sweetcorn and put into a food processor with the spring onions, garlic and semolina. Blitz to a speckled primrose mush; unless you have a big processor you may have to do this in two batches.

3　Tip this mixture into a large saucepan, add the hot vegetable stock and bring to the boil, then turn down the heat and let the chowder simmer, partially covered for 10 minutes.

4　Meanwhile, spread the tortilla chips out on a foil-lined baking sheet and sprinkle the cheese over. Warm in the hot oven for 5–10 minutes or until the cheese melts over the chips.

5　Ladle the soup into bowls and put a small mound of cheese-molten chips into the middle of each bowl. Sprinkle some of the red chilli on top, if you feel like it, and serve immediately to very grateful people.

Serves 6

QUICK CHILLI

I suppose this is more Tex Mex than just Mex, but none the worse for that. Besides, there is a reason why old-fashioned cookery books devoted so much energy to minced meat: it makes for a simple, speedy supper.

Luckily, there is a lot more going for this than efficiency. It just hits the spot when you want something comforting but not bland: it soothes but it's sprightly.

If you've got a rice cooker – and I make no secret of my dependence here – then put your rice in to steam before you make the chilli, and a substantial supper is mere minutes away, which is just the way it should be.

150g chorizo sausage (not the salami sort), halved lengthways and cut into 5mm half moons
500g minced beef
$1/2$ teaspoon ground cumin
$1/2$ teaspoon ground coriander
$1/2$ teaspoon ground cinnamon

3 cardamom pods, bruised
1 x 500g jar good-quality tomato and chunky vegetable sauce for pasta
1 x 390g can mixed spicy beans
60ml sweet chilli sauce
$1/4$ teaspoon chilli flakes (optional, or if your canned beans are not spicy)

1 Put the sliced chorizo into a hot, heavy-based pan and cook over a medium heat until the sausage crisps a little and gives up its orange-red oil.

2 Add the mince and cook for about 5 minutes, breaking it up with a wooden fork to help it brown.

3 Stir in the spices and then add the tomato-vegetable pasta sauce, spicy beans and chilli sauce. Also add the chilli flakes if you need more heat or if you've managed only to find some regular canned beans.

4 Bring to the boil and then turn down the heat and simmer for 20 minutes.

5 You can eat this with rice or just as it is. If you're not adding any rice, you might consider dolloping with a blob of sour cream and sprinkling some grated cheese and chopped coriander. I can't think of a way of eating this that isn't good.

Serves 4

CHOPPED CEVICHE AND MEXICOLA

I don't deny that chopping the fish into such tiny pieces seems against the express ethos, but there's no logic that can dissuade me. Besides, it really means that you hardly have to steep the fish in the acidy juices at all before it is "cooked" or rather denatured (yes, that's the term) by the lime. Not that this is my reason: I find that eating big chunks of raw fish, no matter that it is cured in its acid bath, can spook people out, whereas this dainty confetti somehow doesn't. I am mad for it and, truth to say, really love it with a big bowl of tortilla chips on the side, but for elegance often produce little toasts or tostadas instead. I get a slender French stick or *ficelle* loaf and cut into thin slices; one loaf should yield about 40 mini tostadas. Brush with a little oil and then burnish slightly in a hot oven (200°C/gas mark 6) for 10 minutes.

Use whatever firm white fish is available to you; my Mexican sources speak of *sierra* but that's not an option for me, geographically. If I find black cod, sometimes called Chilean sea bass (and is neither cod nor bass), then I use that, otherwise monkfish.

My Mexicola cocktail goes well with this. I can't say I have a rigid formula for this simple drink: I just pour. But I'll jot down what I usually do, per glass, just to get things straight. I put a shot of Tequila into a glass, top with ice cubes and add lots of lime slices, then fill the glass with very cold Coke or Pepsi.

250g skinless and boneless black cod or monkfish fillet, chopped as finely as you can
1/2 teaspoon dried oregano
1 teaspoon Maldon salt or 1/2 teaspoon table salt
80ml lime juice
3 spring onions, finely chopped

1 jalapeño chilli pepper or any medium-sized green chilli, deseeded and chopped to give 1 tablespoonful
4 x 15ml tablespoons chopped coriander, plus a little more for sprinkling
tostadas or tortilla chips to serve

1 Put the chopped fish in a wide, shallow dish and sprinkle with the oregano, salt and lime juice. Leave this for 8 minutes.

2 Drain the fish, and discard its white milky liquid. Add the spring onions, chilli and coriander to the fish and stir gently together.

3 You can either put teaspoonfuls onto little toasts and sprinkle some more coriander on top, or put the ceviche into a bowl for everyone to dip tortilla chips into.

Makes enough for approx. 40 little tostadas

QUESADILLAS

I have been won over to the way of the wrap generally, but I insist this is the best use of the tortilla ever. I came across it first in Miami, in the Raleigh Hotel in South Beach to be precise. The restaurant there is one of my favourites: it nestles in a ludicrously beautiful garden, hung with shimmering lights; and the food is so good that when I'm in Miami I don't dare eat anywhere else.

The Raleigh's Morning Quesadilla is a tortilla wrap, folded around avocado and scrambled egg, then grilled, and shouldn't by rights be as good as it is. You can do a version of it, should you have any Mexican Scrambled Egg left over from the recipe on page 230, but I find whenever I put avocado in, it squelches out before I get the wrap to my mouth.

These cheese and ham babies are very good to offer alongside the cool ceviche on the previous page, but I often make them for supper. They're that good – and that easy.

I give quantities for each round soft flour tortilla; each quesadilla makes three little triangles and it's really up to you how many of them to eat. I wouldn't presume …

FOR EACH FLOUR TORTILLA WRAP
30g thinly sliced cured ham
3 coin-sliced slices of pickled green
    jalapeño chilli peppers from a jar
50g grated cheese

1 spring onion, finely sliced
few leaves of coriander
1 teaspoon olive oil (not extra virgin)

TO SERVE
good shop-bought salsa of your choice

1 Heat a ridged griddle.

2 Place the tortilla wrap on the counter in front of you and cover with the ham.

3 Over one half only, sprinkle the pickled jalapeño slices, grated cheese and chopped spring onion. Scatter the coriander leaves over the top.

4 Carefully fold the tortilla wrap in half, that's to say, fold the un-cheese-topped half over the cheese so that you have a fat half moon.

5 Lift this up carefully and brush each side with the oil before putting it on the hot griddle; grill for a minute each side.

6 Using a steady hand and a wide fine spatula or fish slice, transfer the tortilla to a board or plate and cut into 3 triangles. Eat with some salsa on the side. And please feel free to play with the fillings as you wish.

Makes 1 quesadilla

ROQUAMOLE

I have practically had to sit on my hands to stop myself writing about this before now. Naturally, I know Roquefort does not come from Mexico, but it melds so deliciously with avocado that I couldn't resist; no more, I hope, will you. And although I have called this incredible dip roquamole, I think it may be better made with a less illustrious *bleu*. St Agur out of a wedge-shaped packet is the blue cheese I keep in the fridge so that I am ever-ready to make this.

You don't need to serve subfusc blue corn tortilla chips with this; you don't have to serve any kind of tortilla chip with this: though both do add to the luscious eat-me quality. But I'm also very keen on a huge platter of dippable bits: radishes, carrot batons, sugar-snaps, you name it.

For me, this can be a dip with drinks, a quick treat for lunch or a greedy solitary dinner. The only meal I've yet to eat it at is breakfast. I think it's just a question of time …

125g Roquefort or St Agur
60ml sour cream
2 ripe avocados
35g sliced pickled green jalapeño
    chilli peppers from a jar

2 spring onions, finely sliced
$^1/_4$ teaspoon paprika
1 packet blue corn tortilla chips

1 In a bowl, crumble or mash the blue cheese with the sour cream.

2 Mash in the avocados. If they are ripe, a fork should be all you need.

3 Roughly chop the sliced jalapeños and stir them into the mixture along with the finely sliced spring onions.

4 Arrange in the centre of a plate or dish, dust with the paprika and surround with tortilla chips. Dive in.

Serves 4–6

FLAN

This is a ridiculous simplification of a traditional Mexican pudding that is no less delicious for being easier to make. You don't always have to suffer for your art.

In effect, this is a large crème caramel; there's nothing to stop you making it as many smaller, individual ones, but it will take longer to line each mould. Why give yourself the work? The fact that the flan takes around 45 minutes to cook doesn't bother me. You don't need to be doing anything while it bakes and, anyway, it needs a good long time to sit around and chill. You can do likewise while that's happening.

The traditional method is to make a kind of milk reduction; I know that opening cans might not be your thing but, in essence, you've just let someone else reduce the milk for you. I find this particular combination of unsweetened evaporated milk and sweetened condensed milk does the trick, so discard your prejudices and arm yourself with your can opener.

A Mexican camera assistant, Luis, I worked with once says this is as good as his mother's. I only hope his mother doesn't know.

150g sugar
1 x 340g can evaporated milk
1 x 397g can sweetened condensed
  milk

3 eggs
2 teaspoons vanilla extract

1 Preheat the oven to 170°C/gas mark 3 and put a kettleful of water on to boil.

2 Put the sugar into a heatproof, heavy-based, or ideally copper, tarte Tatin dish (24cm diameter), and place over a low heat until the sugar begins to turn into a liquid syrup. Swirl the sugar every now and then as it melts.

3 The sugar will begin to caramelize – just before the sugar reaches the colour of maple syrup, take the pan off the heat and place it on a cool surface. While the pan's cooling down a bit, swirl the caramelized sugar a little up the sides of the dish before it sets.

4 Empty the evaporated and condensed milks into a bowl and whisk in the eggs and vanilla extract.

5 Pour this mixture into the syrup-lined tarte Tatin dish and put it in a roasting tin. Fill the tin with freshly boiled water to a depth of about 2.5cm.

6 Bake for 45–50 minutes, or until firm and set. Lift the dish carefully out of its water bath and leave to cool.

7 Leave the flan in the fridge overnight or for 4 hours. When you are ready to serve, turn the flan out onto a dish with enough lip on it to stop the syrup running off.

Serves 8–10

Margarita Ice Cream

This is a cinch to make, and easy-easy-easy to eat. It is a no-churn version of the Margarita Ice Cream in *Forever Summer*. If you want to serve it in glasses with rims dipped in sugar and salt, by all means do. But it is so good that, even as someone who is not a committed ice cream eater and no kind of a drinker, I find I can spoon it straight into my mouth from the container it's chilled in.

In other words: no decorative touches or embellishments are remotely needed. This is truly the express way to dessert-deliriousness.

125ml lime juice
2 x 15ml tablespoons Tequila
3 x 15ml tablespoons Cointreau or
    Triple sec

150g icing sugar or powdered sugar
500ml double cream

1 Pour the lime juice, Tequila and Cointreau (or Triple sec) into a bowl and stir in the sugar to dissolve.

2 Add the cream and then softly whip until thick and smooth but not stiff.

3 Spoon this into an airtight container to freeze overnight. This ice cream does not need ripening (softening before serving), as it will not freeze too hard and melts speedily and voluptuously.

Serves 6

BUÑUELOS

A *buñuelo* is a small fritter of intense fabulousness. I think anything that is fried starts off with an advantage in the taste department, and a good sprinkling of sugar at the end can only help things further.

Although these are fried, they are incredibly light, and the oil you cook them in is very hot, so that the *buñuelos* do not have even the suspicion of greasiness about them.

If you have a freestanding mixer – which generally greatly aids the express life – these are very quick to make, and they take hardly any time to fry. I love them at the end of a meal with a small, hot cup of coffee.

If you want to take an even more express route, simply cut some soft corn tortillas into triangles, deep-fry them quickly but ferociously and then sprinkle with a goodly dusting of icing sugar.

60ml milk	1 x 15ml tablespoon vegetable
1 egg	shortening
150g flour	cooking oil for frying
1 teaspoon baking powder	icing sugar for decorating
1/8 teaspoon cream of tartar	

1 Whisk the milk and egg in a jug.

2 Put the flour, baking powder and cream of tartar into a bowl, rub the vegetable shortening into the mixture either by hand or with a freestanding mixer

3 Pour in the whisked milk and eggs and mix to make a silky dough; be prepared to add a tablespoon extra of flour if it's too sticky.

4 Pour the oil into a pan up to about 2.5cm deep, and place over a high heat.

5 Tear off cherry-tomato-sized balls from the dough, rubbing them between your hands to shape them. Drop into the hot oil and cook for about a minute or two on each side or until golden.

6 Drain on kitchen paper and then arrange on a plate and dust with icing sugar pushed through a tea strainer with a teaspoon.

Makes 30; enough for 4–6, or 8 if just a petit four with coffee

MEXICAN HOT CHOCOLATE

This is not the first of my Mexican hot chocolates, but I feel it will be my last. You can melt chunks of chocolate (as I have in previous versions) into hot milk, but I love the particular richness and thickness you get from good Continental hot chocolate powders. Plus, I add Kahlúa, so there is really no need to consider anything else.

The whipped cream on top is not essential unless you decide to serve this in lieu of pudding-and-coffee, which I can't help thinking is a very, very good idea indeed.

Aerosol cream, which gives that glorious whipped effect is, alas, always longlife, but if you're brave enough, buy a nitrous cream whipper and learn to spurt and squirt the fresh cream at will.

500ml full-fat milk
6 x 15ml tablespoons superior
　　Continental hot chocolate mix
　　(or enough for 500ml liquid
　　according to packet instructions)

4–5 x 15ml tablespoons Kahlúa,
　　depending on taste
squirty cream from a can (optional)
4 long cinnamon sticks

1　Heat the milk in a pan and make the hot chocolate according to packet instructions.

2　Add the Kahlúa and take off the heat before it boils.

3　Serve with a topping of the squirty cream (if using), and put the cinnamon sticks in as you would straws, even though I am not suggesting they be used as such.

Serves 4

On the Run

have never seen any point in claiming to be other than one is and, anyway, I have made the most of being a food obsessive. For good or bad, it's my life, it's me, and I don't see anything changing. Sometimes, though, I have the good taste to be a little ashamed. So, I risk showing myself up in all my foolishness now by confessing that when my son started taking a packed lunch to school every day, I kept a diary, chronicling what I'd given him to eat and – oh yes – memorializing either his comments or the state of his lunchbox at the end of the day. I told myself, I was trying to see what was successful and popular, and what went uneaten.

I realized how madly obsessive I was being when all my friends derided me for charting the princeling's prandial progress like this; not realizing how idiotic I was, you see, I just left the diary in plain sight in the kitchen for ease of jotting.

Well, it didn't last (the abandoned document now languishes in my secret drawer), not just because I was mocked, but also because the novelty wore off, to be frank. But what I did learn is how hard it is to supply decent lunches, or even just something to eat on the hoof, day in, day out, for adults or children, when the food has to travel, sit well and be prepared without major trauma. The recipes that follow represent my attempt to find a way through it all. Just follow me …

PEA AND PESTO SOUP

Providing something hot to eat is the hardest challenge, and although flasks of soup provide scope for spillage and mess, I feel they are worth the risk. This soup – my all-time most-requested – has the bonus, too, of being so simple to make, you can do it while you stumble about the kitchen at breakfast.

While you *can* make it with pesto from a jar, the difference when you use the "fresh" stuff in a tub that you find in chiller cabinets in the supermarkets is astonishing.

I think soups taste better made in a blender rather than a food processor, and it's best to use a blender which has a central plug in the lid that you can remove to stop pressure building up – which, in turn, prevents you getting soup all over you or your walls. That would not be a good start to the day.

750ml water
375g frozen peas
2 spring onions, trimmed but whole
1 teaspoon Maldon salt or
   $^{1}/_{2}$ teaspoon table salt

$^{1}/_{2}$ teaspoon lime juice
4 x 15ml tablespoons fresh pesto
   (from tub not jar)

1 The quickest way to proceed is to fill a kettle first and put it on to boil. When it's boiled, measure the amount you need into a pan and put on the hob to come back to the boil. Fill a thermos with the remaining hot water.

2 Add the frozen peas, spring onions, salt and lime juice to the pan and let everything bubble together for 7 minutes.

3 Discard the spring onions and blitz the peas and their liquid with the pesto in a blender.

4 Empty the thermos flask that you've left filled with hot water and then pour in the soup, making sure you screw the top on securely.

Makes enough for 2 hearty bowls.

CHICKEN CAESAR CORNETS

This is a wrap by another name, but for a reason: there is no way I think a roll-up wrap could survive travel but this, a kind of crêpe-cornet approach is hardier. You'll still have to be careful, but at least you start from an advantage point.

I love these so much, I have to be careful not to eat everyone's packed lunch when I make them.

175g cold cooked chicken, shredded
50g organic mayonnaise (and add
    $^1/_4$ teaspoon crushed garlic to
    taste)
50g flaked Parmesan cheese

100g chopped iceberg lettuce
$^1/_4$ teaspoon Worcestershire sauce
salt and pepper to taste
4 soft corn tortillas

1 Put all the ingredients, bar the tortillas, in a bowl and mix well.

2 Place a tortilla on the counter in front of you and spoon a quarter of your mixture onto one quarter of the wrap. Fold the tortilla in half (by folding the filling-less half over the chicken mixture), and then in quarter, so a flat, double side covers the bulgy, filled side, and proceed with the remaining 3 tortillas. Wrap well with foil before travelling.

Makes 4

Rocky Road Crunch Bars

No one is ever going to complain about having one of these in their lunchbox, and they're pretty handy to have around in the kitchen for a quick, snatched burst of energy at any time.

I'm not claiming them to be a health food, but when you're talking about lunch on the run, packing quite a few calories into a small parcel can be seen as an advantage. That's my view, and I'm sticking to it.

125g soft butter
300g best-quality dark chocolate
    (minimum 70% cocoa solids),
    broken into pieces

3 x 15ml tablespoons golden syrup
200g Rich Tea biscuits
100g mini marshmallows
2 teaspoons icing sugar for dusting

1 Melt the butter, chocolate and golden syrup in a heavy-based saucepan. Scoop out about 125ml of this melted mixture and put to one side.

2 Put the biscuits into a freezer bag and then bash them with a rolling pin. You are aiming for both crumbs and pieces of biscuits.

3 Fold the biscuit pieces and crumbs into the melted chocolate mixture in the saucepan, and then add the marshmallows.

4 Tip into a foil tray (24cm square); flatten as best you can with a spatula. Pour the reserved 125ml of melted chocolate mixture over the marshmallow mixture and smooth the top.

5 Refrigerate for about 2 hours or overnight.

6 Cut into 24 fingers and dust with icing sugar by pushing it gently through a tea strainer or small sieve.

Makes 24

SESAME PEANUT NOODLES

I always make a large vat of these since they're lovely to pick at in the fridge. Plus, although they're easy to make, you do need quite a few ingredients – and this holds true whether you're making a small or big batch, so you may as well go all out.

I buy ready-cooked egg noodles from the supermarket, which make these even faster to fix.

FOR THE DRESSING
1 x 15ml tablespoon sesame oil
1 x 15ml tablespoon garlic oil
1 x 15ml tablespoon soy sauce
2 x 15ml tablespoons sweet chilli sauce
100g smooth peanut butter
2 x 15ml tablespoons lime juice

FOR THE SALAD
125g mangetout
150g beansprouts, rinsed
1 red pepper, deseeded and cut into small strips
2 spring onions, finely sliced
2 x 275g packets or 550g ready-prepared egg noodles
20g sesame seeds
4 x 15ml tablespoons chopped fresh coriander

1 Whisk together all the dressing ingredients in a bowl or jug.

2 Put the mangetout, beansprouts, red pepper strips, sliced spring onions and the noodles into a bowl.

3 Pour the dressing over them and mix thoroughly to coat everything well.

4 Sprinkle with the sesame seeds and chopped coriander and pack up as needed.

Serves 8

BANANA BUTTERSCOTCH MUFFINS

A great portion of my life is spent baking with bananas. I don't know that I would have chosen this path, but since I haven't been able to shake off my inability to throw food away, ever, I am ineluctably driven to find ways of salvaging bananas too ripe to be easily eaten raw. It's hard to resist the lure of these muffins, and they are incredibly quick and easy to mix up and bake. Furthermore, their resilient squidginess makes them very good travellers.

White chocolate morsels can be used in place of the butterscotch ones and my children seem to love both with equal fervour, though I'm pretty fond of these with dark chocolate chips, too.

3 very ripe bananas
125ml vegetable oil
2 eggs
250g flour
100g caster sugar

$^1/_2$ teaspoon bicarbonate of soda
1 teaspoon baking powder
150g butterscotch (or chocolate)
    morsels

1 Preheat the oven to 200°C/gas mark 6 and line a 12-bun muffin tin with muffin papers.

2 Mash the bananas and set aside for a moment.

3 Pour the oil into a jug and beat in the eggs.

4 Put the flour, sugar, bicarbonate of soda and baking powder into a large bowl and mix in the beaten-egg-and-oil mixture, followed by the mashed bananas.

5 Fold in the butterscotch morsels, then place equal quantities in the prepared muffin tin – I use an ice cream scoop and a spatula – and bake in the oven for 20 minutes.

Makes 12

CRUNCHY SALAD WITH HOT AND SOUR DRESSING

As with the Sesame Peanut Noodles (page 261), this is one of those salads I love to have around to pick at from the fridge, and, unlike the noodles, it is the very model of low-cal virtue. But because it's got such powerful flavours, and such bite, it feels more filling and substantial than it has the right to be. It really keeps you going till the next meal, which can be useful halfway through a long day at work.

FOR THE DRESSING

1–2 teaspoons tom yam paste
   (according to taste)
1 teaspoon sesame oil
2 x 15ml tablespoons rice vinegar
1 teaspoon honey
2 x 15ml tablespoons canola oil
sprinkling of Maldon salt or pinch of
   table salt

FOR THE SALAD

125g broccoli, cut into florets or small
   (2.5cm) pieces
125g fine beans, each bean cut into 4
125g baby corn, each cob cut into 4
75g button mushrooms, sliced
100g finely shredded Chinese leaf
   lettuce
150g beansprouts

1 Whisk together the dressing ingredients in a measuring jug.

2 Cook the broccoli florets with the fine beans and baby corn for 2 minutes in a pan of boiling water. Drain and refresh by plunging them into a sink or tub of cold water.

3 Put the shredded lettuce, beansprouts and sliced mushrooms into a bowl and add the drained and refreshed vegetables.

4 Dress the salad, tossing everything together well.

Serves 4–6, depending on whether you're eating this as lunch in its entirety or as a side dish

LUNCHBOX TREATS

This is exactly what it says in the title: crunchy, crisp, sweet and toothsome, and the really great thing is that, as a parent, you feel you are doing your child some good at the same time as giving him or her a treat. The amount of milk chocolate is scant, and I get a warm rush from considering the nutritional benisons of malt, oats and sesame seeds. And how fabulous that this tastes like a home-made Lion Bar of beloved memory.

50g milk chocolate

150g rice malt syrup

55g butter

60g Rice Krispies

30g cornflakes

40g quick cook oats

75g sesame seeds

1 Melt the chocolate, syrup and butter gently in a heavy-based saucepan.

2 Add all the other ingredients, turning to coat everything well.

3 Using your hands (encased in latex CSI gloves), shape the mixture into walnut-sized balls. You should get about 25; you could also make this using a 12-bun muffin tin lined with muffin papers to get 12 larger cupcakes.

4 Let them set in the fridge for an hour or so, and they will keep quite happily in there for a week of treats.

Makes 25 treats or 12 cupcakes

MORTADELLA PASTA SALAD

I have a certain ambivalence about pasta salads, but find that my emotional see-saw tips ever more in favour of them. Truth is, I used to be scathing. But needs must, and finding them so popular with my children makes me see their virtue.

This one is a favourite at home, though none of my finicky lot want the green bits; if you suffer the same constraints, take out the parsley and leave it for adults to sprinkle optionally.

250g fusilli
2 x 15ml tablespoons extra virgin
  olive oil
2 x 15ml tablespoons lemon juice
1 teaspoon Maldon salt or
  ½ teaspoon table salt
½ teaspoon mild German mustard,
  or similar

1 thick slice (approx. 150g) mortadella,
  diced into 5mm squares
1 x 20g packet curly parsley, finely
  chopped
25g Parmesan flakes
salt and pepper to taste

1 Put a pan of water on to boil, add salt to taste, and then cook the pasta according to the packet instructions.

2 Meanwhile, whisk together the oil, lemon juice, salt and mustard to make the dressing.

3 Drain the cooked pasta and tip it into a large bowl, pour the dressing over the pasta and toss well to coat.

4 When cool, stir in the mortadella pieces, chopped parsley (if using) and Parmesan flakes. Check the seasoning, adding salt and pepper as required.

Serves 4 as a packed lunch

Mini Meatloaves

Make these, eat them and you'll see how glorious they are; I know only too well that they don't look so good. But let's not go into that. I find these not only delicious, but a real boon to boot: I can make up a whole batch, and freeze the ones I don't want to dispense immediately. This is a wonderful timesaver.

These mini meatloaves are best eaten cold, either dunked in mayo, ketchup, brown sauce or mustard, or sliced and made up into sandwiches with the whole fandango of sauces. I sometimes add lingonberry sauce to the mix too. Throw in a gherkin and some pickles and this is lunch nirvana. Don't forget the napkins, though.

500g sausagemeat	2 eggs, beaten
500g minced beef	2 teaspoons Worcestershire sauce
80g quick cook oats	1 teaspoon Maldon salt or
70g A.1. steak sauce	$\frac{1}{2}$ teaspoon table salt

1 Preheat the oven to 200°C/gas mark 6.

2 Combine all the ingredients in a bowl, mixing really well with your hands or a fork.

3 Divide the mixture into 12 balls, and then shape them into mini loaves.

4 Sit the mini meatloaves on a lined baking sheet with space between each and cook in the oven for 30 minutes.

5 You could eat them hot, but best let them cool and keep in the fridge to slice and eat in sandwiches, or to dip in mayo.

Makes 12

SPANISH OMELETTE

There's something about a wodgy golden triangle of potato-and-pepper-filled omelette that makes a packed lunch or picnic feel sunshine-filled and cheering. This is easy enough to make, but you do need to get it done in advance as the hottest you want to eat this is room temperature.

It is often decreed that the only ingredients (other than the eggs of course) proper to a Spanish omelette are onions and potatoes, but I like a little touch of olé red from some chopped peppers. Use either the confetti-dice of caramelized ones that come in jars, or buy a jar of whole flame-roasted peppers and roughly chop them yourself.

I am sorry if this offends – and not only the Spanish – but you could speed this up by using some drained, canned new potatoes instead of cooking real ones.

225g baby new potatoes, halved
4 eggs
75g chopped caramelized or flame-roasted peppers from a jar
3 spring onions finely sliced

75g grated Manchego or Cheddar cheese
1 teaspoon butter
drop of oil
salt and pepper to taste

1   Turn on the grill and let it heat up while you start off the omelette.

2   Cook the new potatoes in boiling water for 15 minutes, until cooked through, then drain.

3   Whisk the eggs in a bowl, add the peppers, spring onions and cheese, and season with salt and pepper, then add the cooked, drained potatoes.

4   Heat the butter and oil in a small, heavy-based frying pan, and, when hot, pour in the omelette mix and cook gently for 5 minutes.

5   By this time, the bottom of the omelette should be set and, rather than turn it, simply sit the pan under the grill for a few minutes to set the top.

6   Turn the omelette upside-down onto a plate to let cool. Don't worry if it feels a little wibbly-wobbly in the middle, as it will carry on cooking as it cools.

7   Once cool, slice into 4 large or 8 smaller wedges.

Serves 4 or more, depending on what else is available

BUTTERMILK ROAST CHICKEN

Buttermilk chicken has long been one of my favourite al fresco summer suppers. My method of choice has usually been to spatchcock a chicken – or rather, many chickens – and then cut them into feisty quarters to pile on serving plates. I've altered this to make cooking speedier and conveying easier, by starting simply with drumsticks. Either way, it goes well with the New Orleans Coleslaw on the following page.

12 chicken drumsticks, approx. 1.25kg total
500ml buttermilk
60ml vegetable oil, plus 2 x 15ml tablespoons
2 cloves garlic, bruised and skins removed

1 x 15ml tablespoon crushed peppercorns
1 x 15ml tablespoon Maldon or 1½ teaspoons table salt
1 teaspoon ground cumin
1 x 15ml tablespoon maple syrup

1 Place the chicken drumsticks in a large freezer bag, and add the buttermilk and 60ml of the oil.

2 Add the bruised garlic cloves to the bag along with the crushed peppercorns and salt.

3 Sprinkle in the ground cumin and, finally, add the maple syrup, then squish everything in the freezer bag around to mix the marinade and coat the chicken.

4 Leave the buttermilk marinated chicken in the fridge, ideally overnight or out of the fridge for at least 30 minutes and up to 2 hours.

5 Preheat the oven to 220°C/gas mark 7. Take the chicken pieces out of the bag, shaking off the excess marinade, and arrange them in a roasting tin lined with foil.

6 Drizzle the 2 remaining tablespoons of oil over the chicken, then roast in the oven for about 30 minutes, or until brown, even scorched in parts, and juicily cooked through.

Serves 6

NEW ORLEANS COLESLAW

This is my accompaniment of choice for the buttermilk chicken in the previous recipe. Indeed, I have even converted fiercely committed anti-coleslawers with it. I can't remember why I call it my New Orleans Coleslaw now (I've been making it, or a version of it, for so long), but I think it has something to do with all the wonderful pecan trees I saw when I was there.

Do serve a potato salad alongside the chicken and coleslaw, if you want: in the picture on page 275 you see some baby new potatoes doused in olive oil, salt and a little lime juice, shaken about in a mustard jar.

1 head white or savoy cabbage, about
   1kg before trimming
2 carrots
2 sticks celery
4 spring onions
200g best-quality store-bought
   mayonnaise (preferably organic)

4 x 15ml tablespoons buttermilk
2 x 15ml tablespoons maple syrup
2 teaspoons apple or cider vinegar
100g pecans, fairly finely chopped
salt and pepper to taste

1 Trim and shred the cabbage, either by hand or with a food processor.

2 Peel and grate the carrots, and finely slice the celery and spring onions.

3 Whisk together the mayonnaise, buttermilk, maple syrup and vinegar and coat the shredded vegetables with this dressing.

4 Season, and toss through the chopped nuts.

Serves 6

Cloudy Lemonade for a Sunny Day

I am thinking that carrying a jugful of lemonade out into the yard or garden counts as portable food; and since I am always, always in a hurry, I am no doubt on the run. You could, of course, pour this gloriously simple, old-fashioned lemonade into a thermos flask and carry it on your way.

If the mood takes you, consider adding a handful of raspberries to the blender goblet to create pink lemonade.

1 litre chilled fizzy water	4 x 15ml tablespoons caster sugar or
2 whole unwaxed lemons, cut into	to taste
eighths	ice cubes

1. Put the water, lemon and sugar into a blender in two batches, and blitz until the lemon is puréed.

2. Strain the lemonade into a jug, pressing down into the sieve, and then pour it into tumblers filled with ice.

Serves 4–6

HOKEY POKEY

I was going to say that this isn't as fun as it sounds, but then I reconsidered. Hokey pokey is a Cornish term for honeycomb, just as the Cinder Toffee in *How to be a Domestic Goddess* is the Geordie version. It is wonderful eaten in golden shards or crumbled into the best vanilla ice cream. You can also use it in place of the Crunchie bars on pages 221 and 222. I include it here as it is the perfect present to take to a dinner party. Better than flowers, as they need to be put into a vase, better than chocolate, which people tend to smile politely at, but put away in a drawer: no one can resist a bit of hokey pokey I've found.

The quantities I've specified don't make an awful lot – enough to fill a little tin 12cm in diameter by 6cm deep – but any more and you'd be sued by your dentist.

100g caster sugar
4 x 15ml tablespoons golden syrup
1¹/₂ teaspoons bicarbonate of soda

1 Put the sugar and syrup into a saucepan and stir together to mix. You mustn't stir once the pan's on the heat, though.

2 Place the pan on the heat and let the mixture first melt, then turn to goo and then to a bubbling mass the colour of maple syrup – this will take 3 minutes or so.

3 Off the heat, whisk in the bicarbonate of soda and watch the syrup turn into a whooshing cloud of aerated pale gold. Turn this immediately onto a piece of reusable baking parchment or greased foil.

4 Leave until set and then bash at it, so that it splinters into many glinting pieces.

Makes 125g

have spent a lot, indeed most, of my adult life pretending to myself that I am Italian. But since I have the misfortune not to be Italian in reality, I must be entitled to some – surely the only one – compensation. And that is, I can play a little fast and loose with Italy's culinary traditions. I respect them, I love them, but what – honestly – would be the point of giving you here the recipes that centuries upon centuries of Italians have been cooking as tradition decrees? Part of me would love to do just that (and I have some plans, simmering away on a back burner for the distant *futuro*), but for now I want to be as faithfully Italian as I can in my reworking of recipes, while not feeling that I have to be slavishly authentic.

This isn't necessarily about cutting corners; one of the great attractions of much Italian cooking is its speed, directness and simplicity. But I do know also that many Italian friends of my generation, and younger, don't cook, feeling that their lives are more frenetic and work-dominated than those of their parents and grandparents. The recipes in this chapter attempt to make Italian food easily manageable, after a long day at the office – and I've used an Italian journalist friend as a guinea pig to ensure that I've succeeded in this, without offending real Italians.

I've twiddled and fiddled a little, because that's what brings cooking alive. I love this sort of food, and playing around with it in the kitchen always lifts my spirits. The hardest thing has been whittling down this chapter so that it doesn't take over the whole book. What follows is the backbone of my repertoire and the recipes I just wouldn't, couldn't live without. Hope you feel the same way.

TUNA AND BEANS

This has always been *the* Italian antipasto, and though you are more likely to come across it as the traditional combination of *tonno* and cannellini, I love the flecked terracotta of borlotti beans, giving you the colours of Tuscany on a plate.

And if you are feeling less formally Italianate in mood, then this makes a simple, speedy supper for two; all I'd want alongside is some good bread.

¹/₂ red onion, finely chopped	2 x 15ml tablespoons extra virgin
4 x 15ml tablespoons lemon juice	olive oil
2 x 400g cans borlotti beans	salt and pepper to taste
250g can best-quality tuna (200g	2 x 15ml tablespoons chopped parsley
drained weight)	to garnish

1 Put the chopped onion into a bowl with the lemon juice and let it steep while you get on with the salad.

2 Drain the beans and rinse to get rid of any gloop, then place in a bowl.

3 Drain the tuna and flake it into the beans.

4 Add the olive oil and some salt to the onion and lemon juice mixture, whisking to make a dressing, then pour it over the tuna and beans and transfer to a serving dish.

5 Fork the tuna and bean salad through, seasoning with salt and ground pepper, and scatter the parsley over; if you want to put this on a plate (rather than a dish) consider strewing the plate with rocket first, or make a leafy border.

Serves 4–6 as a starter or as part of a meal

MOZZARELLA WITH CRAZY GREMOLATA

There are no bad ways of eating good mozzarella. I am perfectly happy just with a spatter of salt and a green glug of olive oil, but this is something special. Gremolata – or gremolada – is the traditional flavouring spritz given to ossobuco, and is a sprinkly mixture of grated lemon zest, garlic and parsley. Mine, here, is an exuberant, madcap version, full of fire and flavour and vibrant against the milky white of the mozzarella.

2 balls buffalo mozzarella
1 long red chilli, deseeded and finely
    chopped
6 black olives, finely chopped
zest of 1 unwaxed lemon
$^1/_2$ clove garlic, crushed

$^1/_2$ teaspoon Maldon salt or
    $^1/_4$ teaspoon table salt
3 x 15ml tablespoons extra virgin olive
    oil
2 x 15ml tablespoons fresh parsley,
    finely chopped

1 Slice the mozzarella into 5mm-thick rounds and arrange on a plate.

2 In a bowl mix the chopped chilli with the chopped olives, lemon zest and crushed garlic.

3 Tip in the salt, oil and parsley and stir together to make your c-c-c-c-razy gremolata.

4 Spoon the gremolata down the centres of your slices of mozzarella.

Serves 6 as part of a starter

PAPPARDELLE WITH ESCAROLE

This is as simple and as basic as a recipe could be, and all the better for it. I love the way Italians cook greens with their pasta, and often those are the recipes, perhaps thought to be unglamorous, that rarely make it out of Italy. And maybe it's also the case that non-Italians need a little more persuasion to bung a lettuce in their saucepan. If you can't get escarole, which is a member of the endive family, use any similar lettuce – curly endive, frisée or similar. You want a robust leaf with an edge of bitterness, and with it an equally robust pasta. I always go for the thick, rough ribbon of pappardelle but, failing that, you might consider rigatoni.

1 x 15ml tablespoon garlic oil
1 teaspoon dried chilli flakes
1 large head escarole, roughly sliced
250ml white wine
250ml water
500g egg pappardelle

20g fresh parsley, chopped
50g flaked Parmesan
salt and pepper to taste
1 long red chilli, deseeded and finely
    chopped (optional)

1 Put a large pan of water on to boil for the pappardelle.

2 In another – wide – pan, heat the oil gently with the dried chilli flakes, then add the sliced escarole, stirring to wilt it down in the oil.

3 Add the wine and water and partially cover the pan, letting the escarole cook, bubbling away, for about 6 minutes, while the pasta cooks in its own pan.

4 Toss the drained pasta into the cooked escarole (this will be a fairly liquid mixture), scatter with the parsley and flaked Parmesan and check the seasoning; decorate the top with the fresh red chilli if you want enhanced heat and colour.

Serves 4–6

Linguine with Lemon, Garlic and Thyme Mushrooms

This is one of my proudest creations and, I suppose, a good example of a recipe that isn't originally from Italy, but sits uncontroversially in her culinary canon. I don't think it would be too presumptuous to name this *linguine ai funghi crudi*. It is about as speedy as you can imagine: you do no more to the mushrooms than slice them, steep them in oil, garlic, lemon and thyme and toss them into the hot cooked pasta. I'm afraid this dish had to be forcibly taken away from me during the photo shoot for this book, otherwise I'd have eaten it all up before it could even have its picture taken.

The dressed mushrooms also make a great salad, in which case boost the quantities of sliced mushrooms to 375g (omitting the pasta altogether but keeping the other ingredients the same).

If all you can find is regular button mushrooms, this pasta is still worth making – so no excuses.

225g chestnut mushrooms
80ml extra virgin olive oil
1 x 15ml tablespoon Maldon salt or
    1¹/₂ teaspoons table salt
1 small clove garlic, crushed
zest and juice of 1 lemon
4 sprigs of fresh thyme, stripped to
    give 1 teaspoon leaves

500g linguine
1 bunch fresh parsley, chopped
2–3 tablespoons freshly grated
    Parmesan, or to taste
freshly ground pepper

1 Slice the mushrooms finely, and put in a large bowl with the oil, salt, crushed garlic, lemon juice and zest, and marvellously scented thyme leaves.

2 Cook the pasta according to packet instructions and drain loosely, retaining some water. Quickly put the drained pasta into the bowl with the mushroom mixture.

3 Toss everything together well, then add the chopped parsley, grated cheese and pepper to taste, before tossing again, and eat with joy in your heart.

Serves 4–6

SPAGHETTINI WITH PRAWNS AND CHILLI

This is what I make for people when I want something that needs no thought, no fuss, no effort but will guarantee instant gratification all round. I keep the prawns in the deep freeze and either defrost them overnight (or more likely from breakfast time till after work) in the fridge, or do a quick thaw job when I get home. The "sunblush" tomatoes are generally stashed in my fridge to spruce up salads, make up a quick sauce or gussy up pasta just like this.

1 x 200g packet frozen cooked
   peeled prawns, defrosted
250g spaghettini
2 x 15ml tablespoons garlic oil
4 spring onions, finely sliced
1/2 teaspoon crushed chilli flakes

200g sunblush tomatoes in
   seasoned oil
125ml white wine or Noilly Prat
50g rocket, roughly torn
handful of flat leaf parsley, chopped

1 Drain the defrosted frozen prawns and leave to one side for the moment.

2 Put copious amounts of water on to boil; when boiling, add salt and the pasta, and cook according to packet instructions, or slightly under.

3 Heat the garlic oil in a large pan (big enough to take the pasta later) and fry the sliced spring onions and chilli flakes for a couple of minutes, then tip in the tomatoes with their oil, and the prawns.

4 When both have warmed through, add the white wine or Noilly Prat and let bubble up. Add the rocket and stir until wilted a little.

5 Drain the pasta when ready, reserving 125ml or so of its cooking liquid, and toss the drained pasta in the chilli-prawn pan.

6 Turn out into a large warmed serving bowl and toss everything again so that all is combined, adding a little of the cooking water if needed, and more oil or garlic oil if you want.

7 Sprinkle with the chopped parsley, and serve.

Serves 4 as a starter, 2 as a main course

BLACK PASTA WITH RED MULLET

While it's true that coloured pasta – even the impeccably authentic black, squid pasta – is eaten very much more out of Italy than within, this recipe is inspired by the most wonderful fish pasta I had one summer at a small restaurant, La Fontanina, on the road that spirals up from Porto Santo Stefano on the Tuscan coast. I tend to make this for supper as a special treat, for two, although if you want to, of course, serve it as a starter, but go light, very light, afterwards.

I use rosé wine, because that's what I drink – clinked with ice and spritzed with soda – throughout summer, but white would be fine, and much more Italian to boot.

I've indicated the pasta I customarily use (and buy from the supermarket) as it is much more tender than the dried squid pasta. But, please, use any tender, thin ribbons of pasta you want. And if red mullet is not available, bream (red or black) is the best alternative. Bass would be a lovely, but expensive option.

2 x 15ml tablespoons garlic oil	good grinding of pepper
2 spring onions, finely sliced	2 tomatoes, halved, deseeded and
250g–300g red mullet (or bream)	chopped into dice
fillets	2 x 15ml tablespoons capers
250ml rosé wine	1 x 15ml tablespoon butter
½ teaspoon Maldon salt or	250g fresh black squid tagliolini
¼ teaspoon table salt	handful of whole basil leaves

1　Put a saucepanful of water on to boil for the pasta.

2　Heat the oil in a frying pan and cook the spring onions for a minute before adding the fish fillets, skin-side down.

3　Turn the fillets over after a minute or two, then pour in the wine and add salt and pepper.

4　Once the fillets are cooked through, which should take about another minute, lift them out and wrap in foil to keep warm.

5　Let the winey pan juices bubble down for about 3 minutes, then tip the diced tomato, capers and butter into the pan and whisk on the heat.

6　Cook the fresh pasta – it will take about 2 minutes – and drain. Put it into the sauce, then toss gently but well.

7　Flake the fish, leaving on some red skin, and tenderly toss through the pasta along with the basil, keeping some leaves to sprinkle over when you serve.

Serves 2 as a main course, 4 as a starter

POLLO ALLA CACCIATORA

This is an old favourite – chicken cooked "the hunter's way" – which grants a certain amount of culinary licence. My version is traditional enough, only speeded up and simplified. The unexpected deviation lies in the addition of a can of cannellini beans, which, in effect, turns it into a quick, one-pot, all-inclusive supper. Having said that, I also adore it – as do my children – with plain steamed rice. Whatever, when I cook this, I know I can count on getting tea on the table from scratch in comfortably under half an hour.

1 x 15ml tablespoon garlic oil	125ml white wine
75g pancetta cubes	1 x 400g can chopped tomatoes
6 spring onions, finely sliced	2 bay leaves
1 teaspoon rosemary, finely chopped	$^1/_2$ teaspoon sugar
500g chicken thigh fillets, each cut into 4 pieces	1 x 400g can cannellini beans (optional)
$^1/_2$ teaspoon celery salt	

1 Heat the garlic oil in a heavy-based pan and fry the pancetta cubes, sliced spring onions and chopped rosemary for a couple of minutes.

2 Add the chicken pieces, stirring well, and sprinkle in the celery salt.

3 Pour in the wine and let it come to a bubble before adding the tomatoes, bay leaves and sugar. Put the lid on and let the pan simmer for 20 minutes.

4 Drain the cannellini beans (if using) and add to the pan. When they have warmed through, too, you are ready to eat.

Serves 4

Lamb Cutlets with Chilli and Black Olives

No one does lamb cutlets better than the Italians and this recipe, which comes to me by way of the great Anna del Conte, is a case in point. The nuggets of pink meat are so tender and flavourful that you just want to gnaw every morsel right off the bone.

I'd keep side dishes plain – maybe some steamed new potatoes and green beans or sugar-snaps – as this needs no attention-seeking embellishment.

And I can't tell you how heavenly these cutlets are, should you be lucky enough (and it's unlikely) to have some left over, snatched straight from the fridge the day after.

12 lamb rib chops
4 x 15ml tablespoons olive oil, plus
    2 tablespoons for frying
3 cloves garlic, peeled and sliced
1 teaspoon dried chilli flakes
1 teaspoon dried oregano

zest and juice of 1 small lemon
1 teaspoon Maldon salt or
    $^1/_2$ teaspoon table salt
15 black olives, pitted and sliced
1 long red chilli, deseeded and finely
    chopped (optional)

1 Layer the rib chops between clingfilm and flatten gently with a rolling pin or mallet. Unwrap and place the chops in a large dish, so that they all fit in a single layer.

2 Pour the 4 tablespoons of oil over the chops and add the sliced garlic, chilli flakes, oregano, lemon zest and juice. Sprinkle with the salt and the olives, then turn the rib chops in the marinade so that both sides are coated.

3 Cover and leave the lamb to marinate for 20 minutes at room temperature.

4 Heat the 2 tablespoons of oil in a large heavy-based frying pan, and add the chops, scraping off the marinade before you put them in the pan. (Reserve the marinade.) Fry them for a couple of minutes a side on quite a high heat so that they take on some colour.

5 Turn the heat down to medium and pour the reserved marinade into the pan over the now coloured chops. Add 2 tablespoons or so of water and cook for about 5 minutes for rare cutlets or a little longer if you like your lamb well done (this will also depend on the thickness of the chops).

6 Transfer the chops to a serving plate, pour over the juices from the pan and sprinkle with the chopped red chilli, should you feel like enhancing the dried chilli with the pep of fresh.

Serves 4

LIVER WITH BACON AND CHARRED ONIONS

Liver is not for everyone, I admit, and I wouldn't advise cooking it for a dinner party. But those who like it, adore it, and it makes a great supper treat for two. Liver and onions is as Italian as it is British (though very different) and I add bacon to this, as the salty juices are the perfect frying medium for the liver, adding foil and counterpoint to its moussy, sweet flesh. I like to keep the tones beautifully sombre; with the scorched dark pink of the bacon are splintered sweet strands of blackened red onion, and with the liver – as homage to *fegato alla veneziana* and because the fresh bitterness is just what's needed – I make a salad of maroon-leaved *radicchio di Treviso*.

If you feel like enhancing the Renaissance painting atmosphere, scatter some pomegranate seeds on top.

4 rashers streaky bacon	2 x 15ml tablespoons balsamic vinegar
1 teaspoon garlic oil	2 x 15ml tablespoons water
1 small red onion, peeled and finely	1 x 15ml tablespoon chopped parsley
sliced into half moons	
350g very thinly sliced calves liver	
(about 4 long thin pieces)	

1 Cook the bacon in the garlic oil until very crisp, remove the rashers to kitchen paper to drain and then wrap in foil, forming a baggy but tightly sealed parcel.

2 Cook the onions in the same pan – in the rendered bacon fat – until soft and beginning to char in parts, then remove them to a bowl.

3 Cook the liver in the same pan, for about $1^1/_2$ minutes a side or longer if not very thinly sliced.

4 Divide the cooked liver between 2 plates and quickly deglaze the pan with the balsamic vinegar and water, letting it bubble up and make a scant syrup.

5 Pour this syrup over the liver and cover with the onions. Crumble the bacon over and sprinkle with the parsley.

Serves 2

Italian Sausages in Hot Tomato Sauce with Polenta

Italian sausages are fabulously quick to cook – and fabulously good to eat. And if the lamb chops on page 299, provide just the right sort of heat for a spring or summer meal, these sausages blanket you with winter warmth. This comes from a couple of jars of really top-quality tomato and chilli pasta sauce. A regular pasta sauce just won't cut it here; it has to be a genuinely impressive high-end one.

1 x 15ml tablespoon chilli oil
1kg Italian sausages
4 x 15ml tablespoons Marsala
2 x 340g jars tomato and chilli sauce
    for pasta
250ml water

500g instant polenta
boiling water and chicken stock
    concentrate or cubes (to cook
    polenta)
2 x 15ml tablespoons olive oil

1 Heat the chilli oil in a pan and add the sausages, letting them fry for about 5 minutes until they are coloured.

2 Add the Marsala, let the pan bubble for a minute or so, then pour the tomato chilli sauce and 250ml water over the sausages.

3 Simmer for 15 minutes while you make up the instant polenta according to packet instructions but using chicken stock (from a cube or concentrate) rather than plain boiling water.

4 When the polenta is cooked, whisk in 2 tablespoons olive oil, divide the polenta between 6 warmed plates and top with sausages and hot tomato sauce. If you have more sauce than you need per plate, just pour it into a little jug for people to top up as they want.

Serves 6

Marsala Honey Pears with Gorgonzola

With all due respect to De Gaulle and his countrymen, I would happily forgo each and every one of France's 246 cheeses for one wodge of Gorgonzola. For me, it is the king of cheeses, the queen, the grand empress of cheeses. This dish is my way of paying respects to it, although I am perfectly happy to eat it all alone (both me and the cheese). If you want cheese at the end of a dinner party, then this is the way to do it.

And while it's not an Italian recipe, it is entirely Italian in inspiration. For me it's Autumn in Milan cast in food.

2 x 15ml tablespoons olive oil
(not extra virgin)
2 pears (approx. 500g total weight),
unpeeled and uncored
3 x 15ml tablespoons Marsala

2 x 15ml tablespoons honey
50g walnut halves
500g ripe Gorgonzola in perfect
condition (it should never have
seen the inside of your fridge)

1 Let the oil heat in a large frying pan, while you cut the pears into eighths – i.e. quarter them and halve each quarter.

2 Fry the pears for 3 minutes a side, and, while they are frying, whisk the Marsala and honey together in a cup.

3 When the pears have had their time, throw in the Marsala-honey mixture and let it bubble up vociferously around the pears, then transfer them, all bronzed and syrupy, to a plate.

4 Add the walnut halves to the dark juices left in the pan and stir-fry them for about a minute until they are themselves darkened in part and sticky all over. Remove them to the plate with the pears and add Ingredient X, your Gorgonzola.

Serves 6–8

Peaches in Muscat

The Italians have a way of making a special pudding out of unmessed-up simple ingredients. It's something to do with their touch. Take *affogato*, which is just a scoop of vanilla ice cream "drowned" by having a strong hot cup of espresso thrown over it. Or there's *sgroppino*, which is a scoop of lemon sorbet in a glass (with a couple of optional shots of vodka), topped up with a fizzy hit of Prosecco. Pudding can be entirely shop-bought and still feel like a treat: you just buy a bottle of Vin Santo and provide cantuccini biscuits to dunk in.

And I love the way they make fruit special too, just by washing grapes, cherries, apricots, and sitting them in bowls of iced water directly on the table. This recipe is scarcely more work, and if you don't want to do any of it in advance, just put a bottle of muscat wine on the table and a bowl of peaches, then give everyone a sharp knife and a glass and let them pour their own muscat and slice in their own peaches.

4 ripe peaches
250ml sweet muscat or other good dessert wine
double cream or ice cream for serving (optional)

1 Over a bowl (to catch juices) cut each peach into slices.

2 When all the peaches are sliced, pour in the muscat wine and make sure the peaches are more or less fully immersed. Cover the bowl with clingfilm and refrigerate for up to 6 hours; sometimes it helps to be able to get stuff done in advance.

3 Remove the peaches to a pretty glass bowl or to individual small glasses and serve – still chilled – with a jug of double cream or some vanilla ice cream alongside.

Serves 6

AMARETTO SYLLABUB

This is an Anglo-Italian hybrid: the syllabub is entirely English, though the liqueur makes it Italian in the extreme. The crumbled amaretti biscuits give a trifle-like contrast of soaked sponge and soft cream. Utterly delicious, and the work of moments, this is something you can pull out any time you want to end a dinner party with aplomb.

80ml amaretto liqueur
25g caster sugar
1 x 15ml tablespoon lemon juice

250ml double cream
1 x 250g packet *amaretti morbidi*
(soft almond macaroons)

1 Pour the amaretto liqueur into a bowl with the sugar and lemon juice and whisk to mix.

2 Whisk in the double cream and whip this mixture until thickened but still soft and billowy.

3 Crumble 2 amaretti biscuits into each of 4 glasses (each with a capacity of about 150ml).

4 Divide the syllabub between the glasses, spooning it on top of the crumbled biscuits.

5 Crumble another biscuit or two, and sprinkle this golden rubble over the top of the syllabub in each glass. Serve the remaining amaretti biscuits alongside the syllabub.

Serves 4

BUDINO DI CIOCCOLATO

This is chocolate pudding by another name, though somehow it sounds better in Italian. But frankly, language is irrelevant here: we're talking pure, all-encompassing bliss. When you eat it cooled, it is like chocolate satin cream and almost shocking in its pleasurable intensity. But I love it straight out of the pan, too, when it is like the best hot chocolate you've ever had, in spoonable form. And the spoon you can see overleaf (page 313) is itself chocolate. As Mae West once said, 'Too much of a good thing can be wonderful.'

250ml full-fat milk
125ml double cream
60g caster sugar
1 x 15ml tablespoon cornflour
35g cocoa powder

2 x 15ml tablespoons boiling water
2 egg yolks
1 teaspoon vanilla extract
60g dark chocolate (minimum 70% cocoa solids), finely chopped

1 Put the kettle on, and warm the milk and cream together in a saucepan or in a bowl in the microwave.

2 Put the sugar and cornflour into another saucepan and sieve in the cocoa powder. Add the 2 tablespoons of boiling water and whisk to a paste.

3 Whisk in the egg yolks, one at a time, followed by the warmed milk and cream, then the vanilla extract.

4 Scrape down the sides of the pan and put it on a lowish heat, cooking and whisking for about 3–4 minutes until the mixture thickens to a mayonnaise-like consistency.

5 Take off the heat and whisk in the finely chopped chocolate, before pouring into 4 small cups or glasses, each with a capacity of about 150ml.

6 Cover the tops of the cups or glasses with clingfilm, letting the clingfilm rest on the chocolate surface, to stop a skin forming, and refrigerate once they are cooler. Make sure they are not still fridge-cold when you serve them. You can add a blob of cream on top if you like. And see the biscuits on the next page.

Serves 4

CHOCOLATE MACAROONS

You don't have to serve these *amaretti scuri* with the Budino di Cioccolato but I had to do something with the egg whites left over from the pudding and this is it. I love these macaroons so much that I gladly make them without that excuse, though. They are heady with chocolate, gorgeously chewy and, all in all, dangerously addictive. Luckily (or not, depending on your point of view here) they are quick and easy to make.

2 egg whites
200g ground almonds
30g cocoa powder
175g icing sugar

1 Preheat the oven to 200°C/gas mark 6 and line a baking sheet with parchment paper or preferably Bake-O-Glide.

2 Mix egg whites (unbeaten) with the ground almonds, cocoa powder and icing sugar until you have a sticky but cohesive mixture.

3 Fill a large bowl with cold water and dip your hands in to wet them before rolling the mixture into little balls the size of small walnuts. You will probably have to redunk your hands to keep wetting them as you go.

4 Arrange the macaroon-balls on the lined baking sheet and put in the oven to bake for 11 minutes. It's hard to tell when they're ready, as they will seem squishy but they harden up a little as they cool, and they should be damp within; that's what makes them chewy, so don't worry that the underneaths of the macaroons look sticky.

Makes about 25

There is something about Christmas that seems to instil a piercing fear and quite unparalleled tremor of expectation in people. I can't quite work out whether the greater part is dread or hope – certainly there are components of both – but we seem to feel that for this crucial period we must suddenly become great hosts and untiring chefs, ready with a cocktail and a full table at all hours, at half an hour's notice. That is the kind of person we want to be – oh, and unstressed, smilingly organized and unflappable too. Can this be arranged? Up to a point.

Strangely, this is not the hardest time of the year for the quick cook at all. Obviously, there's no way you can roast a turkey in under 30 minutes, but since I've covered that great central feast at length before, I'll concentrate here on the satellite areas of stress and the related culinary moments. But, first, I do have one quick tip for Christmas Dinner. Instead of making a stuffing for the turkey, buy some good sausagemeat (or I use my favourite Cumberland sausages) from the butcher and, using your hands, wiggle some space between the skin and the breast of the bird and squeeze the sausagemeat in there. In other words, you're stuffing on top of the bird (beneath the skin) rather than inside it. Then, cook it at top volume. You can really blitz the bird as the sausagemeat stops the breast from drying out. Don't mean to boast but I have managed to cook an 8.25kg turkey (and that's minus the weight of the sausagemeat) – in a very hot oven (250°C/gas mark 9–10) oven – in 2^1/$_2$ hours.

But back to the job in hand: I want you to feel better about the big parties, the little dinners that you suddenly find yourself giving without having quite intended to issue the invitation, the meals you end up hosting for stray out-of-towners or distant relatives.

The main trick, if trick it be, is to remember that abundance is the key. And the mood of welcoming plenty can be bought with relatively little effort. The tiring thing would be to try to throw a party that aimed to be the night of a thousand canapés. My mantra has always been "a lot of a little rather than a little of a lot". In other words, choose what you want and make a lot of that, rather than dithering or feeling that you must provide a huge array and many choices, which will only multiply your labours and, in the end, because you'll have less of each, won't look as cosily welcoming.

As in food, so in decoration. At Christmas, I don't like garishness, but I want warmth, and I take the tea-light route. This doesn't have to be expensive: I just put "votive candle" into the eBay search field and then batch-buy cheap. Once you've got a room dotted with red or pumpkin-coloured shot-glass candle holders, each one alight, it doesn't matter if they cost next to nothing each; indeed it's better. And remember, even if each one looks hideous close up, they will look fine en masse. It sounds strange, but that's true.

This time of year, anyway, invites excess, so don't worry about overdoing anything, and just go for it. The only thing that ruins a party is anxiety. But I'm not going to be so irritating as to tell you not to worry: I'm giving you the recipes that will mean you don't have to.

A LITTLE BIT OF THE CHRISTMAS SPIRIT

I certainly don't think you need to offer a choice of drinks at a party, except that you must provide for both those who do and do not take alcohol, but it's good to have a few seasonal cocktails in mind. The Snowball has fallen out of favour, I know, but it's a pity: it could hardly be more seasonal and tastes like grown-up ice cream soda, plus is very much easier to make than eggnog. Christmas in a Glass is just what it says: the smell of the gingerbread syrup as the Prosecco's fizz spritzes it through the air is almost parodically festive. I use the French syrup (Monin's Pain d'Epices) that bartenders have decorating their shelves and I get it online (from www.thedrinkshop.com, a useful source of drinks and syrups), but now there's a coffee shop at pretty well every corner, it's easy to buy the gingerbread syrup they use at this time of year to douse their lattes.

As for the Pomegranate Bellini, this is just Prosecco (or other dry fizzy white wine of your choice) with pomegranate in place of peach purée. If you can't find the pomegranate purée (which, again, I buy online) then do substitute the 100% pomegranate juice you can find a little more easily: it's thinner and less intense, so maybe add a dash of grenadine for a boost. Do not decorate with pomegranate seeds (choking hazard) but consider adorning the serving trays or bar area with pomegranate halves.

Finally, the Rouge Limonade (red lemonade), a drink that is considered not quite *comme il faut* in Paris, but much loved in the countryside. It is really just a spritzer made with red wine, but with lemonade in place of soda. Obviously, don't use really good red wine – and this is why Rouge Limonade can be a major help at a party. You don't want to serve the sort of wine that could double as paint-stripper, but something pretty rough can have its edges knocked off with a generous top-up of lemonade. It's not chic, but it's thirst-quenching – and brightly, seasonally, hued.

SNOWBALL

ice cubes	3 parts chilled lemonade
1 part advocaat	squeeze of lime juice to taste

1 Fill a high-ball glass with ice.

2 Add the advocaat and then top up with the lemonade.

3 Spritz in the lime juice to taste.

1 x 70cl bottle of advocaat should provide for around 14 Snowballs

Christmas in a Glass

4 parts chilled Prosecco, or other fizzy dry white wine
1 part gingerbread-flavoured syrup

1   Pour the Prosecco into wine glasses.

2   Top with the scented syrup.

1 x 75cl bottle of Prosecco should yield 5 glasses

Pomegranate Bellini

1 part chilled pomegranate purée or concentrated juice
3–4 parts chilled Prosecco, or other fizzy dry white wine

1   Pour pomegranate purée into a glass.

2   Top with the Prosecco.

1 x 75cl bottle of Prosecco should yield about 6 Bellinis

Rouge Limonade

3 parts chilled red wine
1–2 parts chilled lemonade

1   Pour the red wine into a tall glass or tumbler.

2   Top with the lemonade according to taste (and quality of wine) much as you would a white wine spritzer.

1 x 75cl bottle of red wine should yield 5 or 6 glasses

Martini Olives

A party has to have bits to pick at, and what could be better than these? I got the idea of Martini Olives from *Dinner For Eight*, a lovely book by Denise Landis, a colleague of mine at the *New York Times*. These aren't just great to have at a party, they're mighty fine to stash in jars and give as presents, too.

> 4 x 240g jars of pimento-stuffed green olives, this gives 550g
> 60ml gin (or vodka if you prefer)
> 1 x 15ml tablespoon vermouth
> 1 teaspoon chilli oil

1. Open the jars and drain the olives, putting them into a bowl with the gin, vermouth and chilli oil, and give them a stir.

2. Leave to steep for half an hour or so while you get ready for your party. (You can put left-over steeped olives back in one of the jars, seal the lid and keep for a couple of days, or longer – though it's doubtful that eventuality will arise.)

Makes 550g olives

Maple Pepper Pecans

I cannot allow myself to have even one of these as I'm setting them out, because I know there will be none left for the party. They're best eaten still a little warm (take care not to serve them too hot or everyone will have a burnt mouth), but are very good cold and, as with the olives, make a nice present, bunged into a jar and tied with a ribbon.

I like the after-hit of fire you get from the cayenne pepper; but if you want these to have a little more universal appeal, substitute mild paprika.

> 50g butter
> 125ml maple syrup
> 1 1/2 teaspoons table salt
> 1 teaspoon cayenne pepper
> 350g pecan halves

1. Melt the butter with the syrup, salt and cayenne pepper in a pan over a gentle heat and add the pecan halves and stir to mix, leaving them on the heat for 2–3 minutes.

2. Spread the pecans on a Bake-O-Glide sheet or piece of foil to cool.

3. Arrange the sticky pecans in bowls to serve.

Makes 350g

Party Popcorn

This is a very speedy, almost comically so, party-eat that is also, obligingly, rather thrifty to make (thus allowing for the extravagance of the pecans on page 319). It's really quite zingy and packed with flavour, and might alarm a passing child expecting more regular sugary fare. But I find that it's hugely popular, which is why I make a substantial batch.

2 x 15ml tablespoons wok oil
200g (un-popped) popcorn maize
50g butter
2 teaspoons ground cinnamon

2 teaspoons ground cumin
2 teaspoons ground paprika
4 teaspoons table salt
4 teaspoons caster sugar

1 Pour the wok oil into the biggest pan you have with a lid, and place over high heat, add the popcorn and quickly put on the lid.

2 Let the popcorn pop, shaking the pan every now and then to keep the kernels moving. You will hear it but don't be tempted to look, unless you want to get shot at, and once it has stopped popping – a couple of minutes or so – take the pan off the heat.

3 Melt the butter with the spices, salt and sugar in another pan, then pour it over the popcorn and put everything into a large paper carrier bag.

4 Shake, shake and shake the bag again to mix the popcorn and get it thoroughly coated in the spicy butter.

5 Arrange in several party bowls.

Makes 3 litres

COCKTAIL SAUSAGES

If you want to have something hot to pass around on a tray, then cocktail sausages are what you're after. There's nothing fiddly to make, nothing to go right or wrong, and everyone loves them. These are not just any cocktail sausages: the sesame oil, honey and soy give them a sweet-savoury stickiness that is pretty well impossible to resist.

1kg (75) cocktail sausages
2 x 15ml tablespoons sesame oil
125ml/150g honey
2 x 15ml tablespoons soy sauce

1   Preheat the oven to 220°C/gas mark 7.

2   Separate the sausages, if they are linked, and arrange in a large, shallow-sided roasting tin.

3   Whisk together the oil, honey and soy sauce and pour over the sausages, then use your hands – or a couple of spatulas – to move everything about in the pan so that all the sausages are slicked.

4   Roast for 25–30 minutes; give them a shuffle about halfway through cooking if you happen to be near the oven.

Makes 75

Halloumi Bites

These are messy to eat and are probably best as part of a table, rather than as a tray-bound snack. If you have the pasta (see next recipe) parked somewhere, perhaps sit this alongside. They go very well together, and eaters can fork up both easily enough. But I wouldn't count these out as finger food, so long as you dole out enough paper napkins. However, since the sausages (see previous recipe) may make babywipes a consideration, anyway, I wouldn't worry unduly.

80ml garlic oil
2 x 15ml tablespoons lime juice
good grinding of pepper

3 x 15ml tablespoons chopped parsley
3 x 250g blocks halloumi cheese,
    drained

1 Combine the oil, lime juice, pepper and parsley in a large shallow dish.

2 Slice the drained halloumi into 5mm-wide pieces, and then cut each slice in half again. Don't worry if bits splinter as you cut.

3 Heat a heavy-based frying pan and dry-fry the slices of cheese, in batches, until golden on both sides – this should take only a minute or so in a hot pan.

4 Put the fried halloumi into the shallow dish containing the other ingredients as you go, and then turn the halloumi about to coat each piece before turning into a serving dish.

Serves 10–12 as part of supper, more as a canapé

FESTIVE FUSILLI

You can think of this either as a soaking-up end-of-party meal for the hard core who manage to stay the course, or as a festive but unfussy supper you can get together quickly after some seasonal get-together or outing. The halloumi on the previous page goes well for either occasion, but the pasta is definitely big and bold enough to be a stand-alone. Should you be lucky enough to have any left over, know that this is a superb post-party breakfast forked straight from a container in the fridge.

By "sunblush" tomatoes, I mean those ones that are halfway between fresh and dried and come soaked in seasoned oil in deli-counters.

600g sunblush tomatoes in seasoned oil	1kg fusilli or other short pasta of your choice
80ml vodka	250g mascarpone
2 teaspoons Maldon salt or 1 teaspoon table salt	40g (2 x 20g packets) curly parsley, chopped
2 teaspoons sugar	flaked Parmesan to serve

1 Put a huge pot of water on to boil for the pasta.

2 Take about 150g of the sunblush tomatoes and chop them finely. I use my mezzaluna here, as you can really mulch them.

3 Put the chopped tomatoes into a bowl with the remaining tomatoes, along with the vodka, salt and sugar. Leave to steep while you cook the fusilli.

4 Cook the pasta according to packet instructions, then drain and put back in the pan with the mascarpone, mixing well over low to medium heat.

5 Tip the steeped tomato mixture and half the chopped parsley into the pan, mixing well together.

6 Pour into a bowl and sprinkle with Parmesan flakes and the remaining parsley.

Serves 10–12

Seafood Pot

In France and Italy, and across much of Continental Europe, seafood is traditionally eaten on Christmas Eve and it is a very good way of embarking on the meat feast that is to follow. But you don't have to stick to the custom, just keep this in mind for a very quick, warming and yet elegant supper. A fennel salad before or after would be lovely, but you need no more with it than just some bread for dunking. Adding the Holiday Hot Cake (see page 344) as a pudding would finish the evening off with gusto, and in suitably festive fashion.

750g palourde clams
750g monkfish fillet
750g salmon fillet
750g cleaned squid
2 x 15ml tablespoons butter
drop of wok oil

125ml white wine
60ml Pedro Ximénez sherry, or other
　rich dark sherry
2 x 15ml tablespoons chopped fresh
　chives (optional)

1 Soak the clams in a bowl of cold water, leave for about 5 minutes while you slice the fish (see 2 below), then discard the open or cracked clams and drain the rest.

2 Cut the monkfish and salmon into 1cm slices, and slice the squid into rings the same width.

3 Warm the butter and oil in a large pot or pan with a lid, then, over a high heat, toss in the fish and squid and stir them around until they begin to go opaque.

4 Add the clams and white wine, then clamp on the lid, shaking the pot over the heat, and let it all cook for about 3 minutes.

5 Lift the lid, avoiding the steam, and pour in the sherry. Cover again and then leave for another 3 minutes or so, shaking it about every now and then.

6 Serve the seafood in the pot, sprinkling with the chopped chives if preferred.

Serves 6–8

BROCCOLI AND STILTON SOUP

At this time of year, it's good to have a thick warming soup at your fingertips and this is plenty seasonal into the bargain. Here's what makes it easy: I use frozen broccoli; actually, frozen organic broccoli, if that makes you feel better. In fact, this is better when made with frozen, and certainly more convenient for an impromptu standby. (The broccoli is frozen fresh, whereas the drooping heads at the bottom of my fridge inevitably end up brassy and brassic.) Moreover, at this time of year my fridge is too full, and it is helpful to have some crucial ingredients stashed in the freezer.

This is also a useful way of turning plain, cold, sliced turkey into a warming meal.

3 x 15ml tablespoons garlic oil
6 spring onions, finely chopped
2 teaspoons dried thyme
1kg frozen broccoli
1250ml hot vegetable stock (from
    concentrate or cube)

200g crumbled or chopped Stilton
freshly ground pepper
1 long red chilli pepper, deseeded and
    finely chopped (optional)

1 Put the garlic oil in a large pan over a medium heat, add the chopped spring onions and cook for a couple of minutes.

2 Add the thyme and the frozen broccoli, and stir in the heat for a minute or so.

3 Add the hot vegetable stock and the crumbled or chopped Stilton and bring to a bubble, then clamp on the lid and cook for 5 minutes.

4 Liquidize in a blender (or failing that a processor) – in batches – then pour back in the pan and heat if it's cooled too much while blending, and add pepper to taste.

5 Scatter with a Christmas confetti of red chilli dice on serving, if you feel like it.

Serves 4 as supper or 8 as a starter

Butternut Squash with Pecans and Blue Cheese

This has many strings to its bow: it serves as a vegetarian alternative to the Christmas turkey; it gussies up a plate of cold leftover turkey; it adds the right balance of mellow warmth and tang to any plain wintry dish; it is a good whole meal on days when you just feel fleshed-out.

2kg butternut squash
3 x 15ml tablespoons olive oil
6 stalks fresh thyme or ¹/₂ teaspoon dried thyme

100g pecans
125g Roquefort or other blue cheese
salt and pepper to taste

1 Preheat the oven to 220°C/gas mark 7.

2 Halve the squash, leaving the skin on, and scoop out the seeds, then cut into 2.5cm cubes; you don't need to be precise, just keep the pieces uniformly small.

3 Put the squash into a roasting tin with the oil. Strip the leaves from 4 stalks of thyme, and sprinkle over the butternut squash. (If you can't get fresh thyme, use dried.) Roast in the oven for about 30–45 minutes or until tender.

4 Once out of the oven, remove the squash to a bowl and scatter the pecans and crumble the cheese over it, then toss everything together gently.

5 Check seasoning and add the last of the thyme, torn into small sprigs to decorate.

Serves 6–8

TURKEY TONNATO

This is a seasonal version (and speedier to boot) of the classic Italian *vitello tonnato*: instead of poaching veal and then making mayonnaise with tuna, I fan out onto a plate some slices of cold turkey, left over from the feast, and quickly whiz up the tuna mayonnaise using really good tuna – the one I like comes in a jar and is from the belly of the beast, called "*ventresca*". Even though my mother's shade would curse me for buying "fresh" mayonnaise rather than making my own, that's what I do here. I wouldn't want any white gloop out of a jar, though.

This is gorgeous with a wintry salad of shredded radicchio; the bitterness offsets the richness of the pinky-buff coloured mayonnaise dressing. If you've got time, a hot baked potato alongside is also, strangely, good.

170g shop-bought fresh mayonnaise
1 x 190g jar best-quality tuna, drained
4 teaspoons lemon juice
5 x 15ml tablespoons sour cream
¹/₂ teaspoon paprika

500–600g cold sliced turkey breast
1 x 15ml tablespoon capers
8 anchovy fillets, each cut in half
   lengthways

1   Put the mayonnaise, tuna, lemon juice, sour cream and paprika into a blender, and whiz to make a sauce.

2   Arrange the turkey slices on a large platter, and then pour the tonnato sauce over to cover most of the turkey slices.

3   Arrange the anchovy fillets in a criss-cross pattern, or however pleases you, and scatter the capers about on top.

Serves 6

SPICED PEACHES

For me, this is an absolute Christmas Must and, as with so many good things in my life, comes to me from my sister-in-arms, Hettie Potter. I've used bottled peaches, I've used canned peaches, and it honestly doesn't matter which, but I'm afraid you have to resist the healthier peaches canned in fruit juice rather than syrup. If you can find only slices, not halves, so be it. This is a beautiful condiment to eat with roast ham, hot or cold, and I love it with cheese, too. It makes the kitchen feel like a proper Christmas kitchen, and it's a very easy present to whip up for people, too – beautiful in old-fashioned glass jars.

2 x 400g cans peach halves in syrup
1 x 15ml tablespoon of rice vinegar or white wine vinegar
2 short sticks cinnamon
1 x 4cm piece of ginger, peeled and sliced thinly into rounds

$^1/_2$ teaspoon dried chilli flakes
$^1/_2$ teaspoon Maldon salt or $^1/_4$ teaspoon table salt
$^1/_4$ teaspoon whole black peppercorns
3 cloves

1 Empty the cans of peaches with their syrup into a saucepan.

2 Add the vinegar, cinnamon, sliced ginger, chilli flakes, salt, peppercorns and cloves.

3 Bring the pan to the boil, and let the contents bubble for a minute or so, then turn off the heat and leave in the pan to keep warm.

4 Serve the peaches with a hot ham, letting people take a peach half each and some of the spiced juice. (Any leftover spiced peaches can, and should, be stored in a jar and then eaten cold with cold ham.)

Serves approx. 8 people with a joint of ham

CHOCOLATE PISTACHIO FUDGE

I am willing to believe that a confectioner wouldn't call this proper fudge, but it tastes divine, and you won't need a sugar thermometer or have to test for frightening soft or hard ball stages. I like this best when it's made slightly less express, but with no greater effort, by stashing it in the deep freeze. It goes really grainy and fudgy this way. If I'm not handing this straight round at a party or with coffee after dinner, I might keep half in my freezer, and put the other half in a box or two for Christmas presents. Make sure they stay cold, though.

350g dark chocolate (minimum 70% cocoa solids), chopped
1 x 397g can condensed milk

30g butter
pinch salt
150g pistachios

1 Put the chopped chocolate, condensed milk, butter and salt in a heavy-based pan on a low heat, and stir to melt.

2 Put the nuts into a freezer bag and bash them with a rolling pin, until broken up into both big and little pieces.

3 Add the nuts to the melted chocolate and condensed milk and stir well to mix.

4 Pour and spatch this mixture into a foil tray 23cm square, smoothing the top.

5 Let the fudge cool, and refrigerate until set. You can then cut it into small pieces approx. 3.5 x 2.25cm.

6 Once cut, it can be kept in the freezer – no need to thaw just eat straight away.

Makes approx. 60 pieces of rich fudge

QUICKLY SCALED MONT BLANC

This is a pared-down, lazy person's Mont Blanc, the traditional dessert of chestnuts, chocolate and cream. Think of it as gastro-geography: crumbled chocolate is the soil; chestnut purée the mountain; cream the snow; and the final scattering of meringue is fresh snowfall. Sounds whimsical, but when something tastes like this you don't care.

If, like me, you cannot have too much chestnut at this time of year, consider doing a variant of the Nutella Pancakes on page 374, replacing the Nutella with sweetened chestnut purée and the Frangelico liqueur with rum. You could substitute broken pieces of marrons glacés for the chopped hazelnuts or you could just as easily leave them out altogether.

> 100g dark chocolate, minimum 70% cocoa solids
> 500ml double cream
> 2 meringue nests (approx. 7–8cm diameter each) from a packet
> 1 x 500g can sweetened chestnut purée or spread, such as Clément Faugier

1 Chop the dark chocolate with a mezzaluna, sharp knife or in a processor until you have rubbly shards. Divide the chocolate between 6 smallish glasses, each with about 125ml capacity.

2 Lightly whip the cream, and crumble and fold through it one of the meringue nests.

3 Dollop the chestnut purée or spread, on top of the chocolate rubble in each glass. Then spoon the cream and meringue mixture over, crumbling a little more meringue on the top of each one.

Serves 6

MINCEMEAT PARCELS WITH BOURBON BUTTER

This is not a time of year when you want to forget the sweet stuff, and this is a fabulous, fast-forward mince pie. You buy a couple of packets of ready-rolled puff pastry, unfurl one sheet, dot with mincemeat, cover with the other unrolled sheet and stamp out squares with a small fluted cutter. Then they go into the oven, though they could sit in the fridge first, if that were helpful to you.

They do spill out like accordions sometimes during baking, but they just need to be pressed back into shape, which is both easy and satisfying. Oh, and the bourbon butter is not an optional extra: it is a reason for living in and of itself. All you do is cream 100g butter with 200g soft light-brown sugar, in a mixer, processor or by hand, and gradually beat in 2–3 tablespoons bourbon, to taste. I've made a lot, because it's very good to have around at this time of year, and not just on Christmas cake or pudding. It's also useful for spreading over any sort of fruit that you might want to blister under a hot grill. Or it may profitably be eaten straight from a spoon.

2 x 375g packets (23 x 40cm sheet) ready-rolled puff pastry, defrosted if frozen
150g superior mincemeat
1 egg

1 Preheat the oven to 220°C/gas mark 7. Carefully unfurl the pastry sheets and lay them out.

2 Using a 4cm square cutter (ours was fluted), outline lightly (don't cut through) one of the pastry sheets with squares, making sure you cover the pastry sheet and line the squares up neatly in a grid with no gaps.

3 Put scant $^1/_2$ teaspoon of mincemeat into the middle of each square.

4 Beat the egg and, with fingertip, outline the edges of the squares with an eggy line.

5 Cover the eggy-lined sheet of pastry with the other sheet, placing it directly on top. Press down at the edges, and then run your fingers down the sides of each square to form a rough outline of bump-filled squares.

6 Using the cutter again, this time cut right through the pastry to make ravioli-type parcels. Make sure they are sealed at the edges before placing the parcels on a lined baking sheet spaced slightly apart.

7 Bake in the oven for 15 minutes. Should they open out like accordions, don't panic. Once they're out of the oven you can squeeze them gingerly back together with the golden lids on top. Let them cool on a rack to a bearable warmth, and serve with bourbon butter.

Makes 35

This is a Christmassy-spiced version of those magic pudding-cakes which look like some sort of joke as you make them, pouring boiling water over batter, but when they've been cooked turn out to be, admittedly unhandsome, sponges with thick sauce underneath. Looks are not everything, and the ginger-butterscotch flavours of sponge and sauce make this a seductive winner. And that's even before we've got on to the eggnog cream. This is a miracle topping that you will want to put on Christmas pudding, hot chocolate, any cake or pie, in fact anything and everything. I see no earthly reason why not.

150g flour	125ml full-fat milk
100g light muscovado sugar, plus 200g extra	60ml vegetable oil
1 teaspoon baking powder	1 egg
2 teaspoons ground ginger	6 teaspoons butter
2 teaspoons mixed spice	500ml boiling water

1   Preheat oven to 220°C/gas mark 7 and place a baking sheet on the shelf. Put water on to boil.

2   Mix together the flour, 100g of the sugar, the baking powder, 1 teaspoon of the ground ginger, 1 teaspoon of the mixed spice, and the milk, oil and egg.

3   Put into a greased, round baking dish (23cm diameter x 6cm deep).

4   In another bowl, mix together the remaining 200g of sugar with the remaining teaspoons each of mixed spice and ground ginger, and sprinkle over the batter in its baking dish. Dot the butter on top and pour the boiling water over the mixture. Trust me.

5   Put the dish on the baking sheet in the oven for 30 minutes. Let stand for 10 minutes before serving, and make sure you scoop out the sauce beneath the sponge in the dish.

Serves 6–8

EGGNOG CREAM

350ml double cream	125ml advocaat

1   Put the cream and advocaat in a bowl.

2   Using an electric whisk, whip until thick but still soft.

3   Serve with Holiday Hotcake, or indeed any festive pud.

Makes approx. 500ml

MARSHMALLOW CRISPY SQUARES

You'd think this was designed to keep the children happy, and while that's OK with me, it is the adults who seem to find this particularly irresistible. But if you can't appeal to the child within at this time of year, when can you?

If I can find a tub of edible disco glitter in one of my cupboards, I sprinkle some on while the marshmallow is still sticky, but it has a certain pearly, luminescent appeal as it is.

It's also beautiful cut into squares, then each piece pierced with a white birthday cake candle, and arranged on a stand. Alternatively, you could turn this into more of a pickable pud, by cutting the slab into teeny-tiny squares so that people can pop one straight into their mouth.

45g butter
300g mini marshmallows
180g Rice Krispies
edible glitter or sprinkles (optional)

1 Melt the butter in a large, heavy-based saucepan over a low heat.

2 Add the marshmallows and cook gently until they are completely melted and blended, stirring constantly.

3 Take the pan off the heat and immediately add the cereal, mixing lightly until well coated.

4 Press the mixture into a greased 32cm x 23cm tin; you may have to put on vinyl CSI gloves and press it down into the corners, as it will be very sticky. Flatten the top and then scatter over the edible glitter or sprinkles, if so inclined.

5 Let the marshmallow crispy squares cool completely in the tin and then cut them into 24 squares.

Makes 24 squares

STEEPED CHRISTMAS FRUITS

I suppose this is the lazy person's Christmas pudding, only that makes it sound like some sort of also-ran, when it is in actual fact rather more of a reward for the time-squeezed and exhausted. Well, we deserve one. I always used to steep dried fruits in brandy, then I moved on to rum, and now I'm firmly settled into a Pedro Ximénez phase. If you haven't tried this rich, dark, raisiny sherry, then I beg you to do so. And, although the suggestion of dolloping dried fruits steeped in it is already a shortcut, I can offer an even speedier solution, which is simply to pour this sherry straight over some vanilla ice cream for an instant, perfect pudding.

My sister Horatia and I have a strict no-presents policy for Christmas (both our birthdays follow straight after) and giving her a jar of liqueur-steeped fruits is my way of getting round the ban.

500g mixed luxury dried fruits (a mixture of raisins, sultanas, currants and glacé cherries)
400ml Pedro Ximénez sherry, or other rich dark sherry, plus some

1 Tip the dried fruit into a 1.25-litre preserving jar, or use several smaller jars.

2 Pour in the Pedro Ximenez; the liquid will more than cover the fruit, and over time the fruit will swell, growing to fill the jar.

3 Leave the fruits for at least a week, although, if you were desperate, overnight would just about do. In either case, make sure you keep topping up with sherry.

4 Eat with vanilla ice cream, or however you want.

Makes 1.25 litres

Seasonal Fruit Salad

This time of year has me foraging about my déclassé drinks cabinet. I've already found very good use for my advocaat and now I can't help reaching for the Tuaca. A Tuscan liqueur, ultra Christmassy, this is rather like a sweet brandy with vanilla and orange; think panettone in liqueur form. I don't expect everyone to keep some at home, though I bought mine easily enough (too easily some might say) and there are worse things than having this about the house just for drinking during the festive season. You can replace it with a mixture of brandy and Cointreau or some sweet, sticky orange liqueur, if that's easier. I wouldn't rule out plain brandy, but, in this case, you will need to double the sugar when making the syrup.

As with the steeped fruits on page 348 (and see the festively combined photograph on page 349), the Express point of this isn't that it can be all done and dusted in five minutes flat – some longer steeping is advised – but that it is NO EFFORT WHAT-SOEVER. This always matters, but it matters now more than ever.

6 satsumas or clementines
250ml Tuaca, or a mixture of brandy
    and Cointreau

100g caster sugar
seeds from 1 pomegranate or 1 x 75g
    tub pomegranate seeds

1   Peel the satsumas or clementines and put the segments into a bowl.

2   Pour the Tuaca over and leave for a couple of hours or overnight.

3   Drain the fruit over a small pan to catch the Tuaca, and then add the sugar to the liquid. Stir to dissolve the sugar, then bring to the boil and do not stir again at all, but let it bubble for 5 minutes.

4   Let the syrup cool slightly, and then pour it back over the satsuma or clementine segments. Add the pomegranate seeds and tumble to mix.

Serves 6–8

Hot Toddy

Although it's true that this is the season of goodwill, it is also the season of colds and chills, and so it is only fair to end with something to take the edge off and generally de-sniffle and uplift.

60ml bourbon (or rum if you prefer) **1 x 15ml tablespoon honey**
60ml water **small paring of lemon zest**
1 teaspoon lemon juice **1 clove**

1 In a small pan, pour the bourbon, water, lemon juice and honey and put on the heat.

2 Stud the shaving of lemon zest with a clove and drop in the pan.

3 When everything's warm, pour into a glass and drink.

Serves 1

get a sense that everyone believes there to be some secret storecupboard rules that, once applied, mean you never have to go shopping again and can cook anything and everything without a moment's thought. It just isn't so, and couldn't be so. What all recipes have in common is that you have to shop for them, and whether the ingredients are recondite or uninspiringly everyday, doesn't make a difference. That is stating the obvious, but I feel it's necessary.

Of course, you can keep an awful lot in stock, and I do. But you have to maintain a balance between having enough food to avoid the need for shopping every day, but not so much that your cupboards are sagging with the weight of cans you hardly ever want. As someone who has a terrible hoarding instinct, I know how useless a full cupboard can turn out to be.

For the truth is, you don't want a diet made up of food that can be kept indefinitely. And even if you did, it wouldn't be good for you. I like to know that I have sufficient supplies to make pasta and sauce for the children without a shopping expedition; that if I buy a roasting chicken, I've got some white beans to mash, along with the garlic or truffle oil to turn it from blah to brilliant; or that if someone drops in unexpectedly, I can construct some sort of pudding I had not planned on; but more than that and I fear I am not filling a storecupboard but building a bunker.

I can certainly give an indication of what I think's helpful to keep on hand; most of these ingredients have already made their presence felt throughout the book. After all, it's impossible to have so many quick and easy recipes without a great deal of reliance on the storecupboard on an everyday basis.

Most of my shortcuts involve **infused oils**, with **garlic oil** in pole position, **wok oil** the next most regularly used, and **chilli oil** coming in third but still most definitely earning a place on the podium. I am relaxed about buying them – and they are readily available in supermarkets – but if you want to make your own, it's not hard. For **garlic oil**, chop up 8 garlic cloves and add to $^1/_2$ litre of regular olive oil, then let it all steep for 48 hours before straining into a bottle (with a funnel, or you'll waste your precious work). For **wok oil**, don't use olive oil but 450ml sunflower or other vegetable oil, plus 50ml toasted sesame oil, 4 sliced cloves of garlic, a 6cm piece of ginger sliced, and strain after the 48 hours' steeping. For **chilli oil**, take $^1/_2$ litre vegetable oil and chop up 4 hot red chillis, and let them sit, seeds and all, in the oil before sieving after 48 hours, as with the other oils. You can pretty well flavour any oil as you wish, and although you don't, strictly speaking, have to sieve out the bits – so long as they are immersed in oil, they shouldn't go off any sooner than ordinary oils – I find it easier to do it at the beginning than have to think about it again.

I always have a barrage of beans and other pulses in the house: this means I have the wherewithal for a vegetable, a starter-salad, a soup or protein for non meat-eaters. I think it's important to use the freezer as an extension of the storecupboard, too. And I don't just mean as a repository of made-up dishes that can be thawed, but for as many vegetables as possible. Don't sniff: the vegetables in your deep freeze are likely to have far more nutrients than the veg lying optimistically at the bottom of your refrigerator.

I could go on, but I don't want to be prescriptive about what you should or could keep in your fridge and on your shelves: just written as a list, it's largely unhelpful. But the recipes that follow provide honest guidance as to what I think can get you out of a jam when you've got people to feed on little or no notice. Good luck!

My Three Favourite Dressings

It's not hard to make a dressing every time you want a salad – and there's nothing wrong with just a spritz of lemon, a shake of salt and a drizzle of fabulous oil straight onto the leaves in the bowl – but I tend to keep my three most-used and most-loved dressings ready shaken-up in jars about the kitchen. I don't store them in the fridge, though no doubt the health and safety police would tell me I should.

These dressings are also a good way of spritzing up plain boiled or steamed veg and can serve as marinades, too, though in that instance, I'd dilute with more oil rather than apply them straight.

Golden Honey Mustard Dressing

This is wonderful on any salad, but particularly good on bitter leaves such as chicory or radicchio. If you can't get hold of rapeseed oil, any oil of your choice will do, although the dressing will be less golden.

4 x 15ml tablespoons Dijon mustard	250ml rapeseed oil
2 x 15ml tablespoons honey	1 teaspoon Maldon salt or
80ml lemon juice	$^1/_2$ teaspoon table salt

1   Put all the ingredients into a jam-jar, make sure the lid's on firmly and shake like mad.

Makes 330ml

Anchovy Red Wine Dressing

Again, this is good on robust bitter leaves, but acts as a glorious contrast to the soft sweetness of grilled peppers. I keep packets of chargrilled peppers in the freezer, which I roast from frozen and then douse in this.

8 anchovy fillets	60ml garlic oil
60ml red wine vinegar	175ml olive oil

1   Put all of the ingredients into a blender, and whiz to make the dressing.

2   Pour into a jam-jar to store.

Makes 295ml

Wasabi Lime Dressing

This beautiful green dressing packs a real punch: I love it on watercress and avocado salad and, indeed, on anything that is served alongside food that is fairly plain, when you welcome the buzz.

3 x 15ml tablespoons lime juice
4 x 15ml tablespoons groundnut oil
1 x 15ml tablespoon wasabi paste from a tube
$^1/_2$ teaspoon Maldon salt or $^1/_4$ teaspoon table salt

1 Put all of the ingredients into a jam-jar, seal tightly and shake to mix.

Makes 105ml

RED PEPPER HUMMUS

You know those days when you had no idea you were having people for dinner and then that phone call comes mid-afternoon? Well, this is the quickly assembled first course that can turn a plain roast chicken, or anything else you think you can stretch to feed four people without much effort, into a dinner party. And, actually, whenever you have to cook with barely time to plan, I think a roast chicken is nearly always the ideal main course: it's much easier to come up with frills for before and after and alongside than to construct a fancy dinner party dish last minute.

This hummus can be dolloped onto crostini (and you can buy baby toasts ready made for the purpose in Italian delis) or eaten as a dip, and it even serves as a rather intriguing, brilliantly hued sauce for plain grilled meats.

1 x 350g jar flame-roasted red peppers
1 x 410g can chickpeas
1 teaspoon paprika
2 x 15ml tablespoons Philadelphia
    cream cheese

2 x 15ml tablespoons garlic oil
1 teaspoon lime juice
salt to taste

1   Drain the peppers and chickpeas and put them into a food processor.

2   Add the paprika, cream cheese, oil and lime juice.

3   Whiz to form a hummus-like purée, and then add salt, and perhaps more lime juice, according to taste.

Makes 500ml

GOLDEN GOAT'S CHEESE

It's always worth keeping your own breadcrumbs around (I have bags of them in the freezer) but I am a total convert to the way of the panko, the Japanese breadcrumb mix you can buy in packets and then, once opened, leave in the freezer to use just as they are; you never need to thaw them.

What makes this recipe a real storecupboard standby is that the little discs of goat's cheese have an unbelievably long use-by date, so you can keep them for emergencies and bring out something really very impressive when the occasion demands.

If you fry the crumb-coated cheese, it will go a deeper gold, but the oven method requires less of you: your choice.

1 egg	30g panko breadcrumbs
good grinding of fresh pepper	4 x 25g (1 packet) goat's cheese rounds

1. Preheat the oven to 220°C/gas mark 7.

2. Beat the egg in a wide bowl with the pepper, and put the breadcrumbs into a wide, shallow dish.

3. Dip the goat's cheese in the peppery egg and then press firmly into the breadcrumbs. You will need to turn the cheese over and press on the other side to coat evenly, and press a little on the sides as well.

4. Sit the breaded goat's cheese on a lined baking sheet and cook for 10 minutes, by which time the cheese will have become gooey inside but will still hold its shape. You can also fry these, and in which case, heat a pan with enough oil nearly to cover the cheeses as they fry. Once the oil is hot they will only need a minute or so each side.

Makes 4

LENTIL AND WALNUT SALAD

There is no need to serve this with the goat's cheese, but the pairing certainly makes for a special starter without much ado.

400g can organic Puy lentils (ready cooked)	4 teaspoons walnut oil
15g chopped fresh chives	2 teaspoons sherry vinegar
50g walnut pieces	salt and pepper to taste
1/2 teaspoon Maldon salt or 1/4 teaspoon table salt	

1. Drain and rinse the lentils and put them in a bowl with the chives and walnuts.

2. Whisk together the salt, oil and vinegar and then dress the salad, stirring well and checking the seasoning.

Serves 2 or 4 with the goat's cheese

SALADE NIÇOISE

Everyone seems to have a very strong opinion as to what should or should not go into a Salade Niçoise, so let me tell you from the outset, I have no desire to join the fray. I put in what I have at home from, broadly, the accepted canon, but not necessarily everything the purists would. Since the tomatoes we get mostly don't have a lot of flavour, I tend to use those tubs of "sunblush" tomatoes, and their intense, flavourful acidity works well here. I am a great believer in keeping these on hand.

Otherwise, speed being of the essence, the only real deviation is that I use croutons (some high-end baked ones from a packet will do) rather than boil potatoes and then have to wait for them to cool.

If there's a single recipe that demonstrates what you can make almost exclusively from storecupboard ingredients, then this must be it.

2 eggs	juice of $1/2$ lemon
100g frozen green beans	$1/2$ teaspoon Maldon salt or pinch of
200g sunblush tomatoes in	table salt
seasoned oil	$1/2$ teaspoon sugar
100g sliced, stoned black olives	40g croutons
1 x 225g jar or can excellent tuna	4–6 anchovy fillets (optional)
250g iceberg lettuce pieces	small handful fresh basil leaves
4 teaspoons extra virgin olive oil	

1 Put the eggs in a panful of cold water, bring to the boil and let bubble for 7 minutes. Three minutes in, add the frozen beans.

2 Drain both the beans and eggs; let eggs sit in a bowl under running cold water, and hold the beans in a sieve just under the tap for a moment, too, so that eggs and beans stop cooking and the beans get cold.

3 Tip the tomatoes and their oil into a bowl, add the olives and mix gently.

4 Arrange the lettuce on a serving dish and then top with the tomato-olive mixture, saving their flavoursome juices in the bowl.

5 Drain the tuna and place chunks of it along with the tomatoes and olives, then strew with the drained beans.

6 Using the reserved juices left in the tomato mixture's bowl, make the dressing: whisk in the olive oil, lemon juice, salt and sugar and pour over the salad.

7 Peel and quarter the almost but not quite hard-boiled eggs and add to the salad along with the croutons, anchovy fillets (if using) and basil leaves.

Serves 2 for supper or lunch, in other words, a substantial main course

MINESTRONE IN MINUTES

This is child's play to make, and I use the term advisedly, since it is the invention of my ten-year-old son Bruno (Brunostrone, we call it) and we make versions of it constantly. Use any beans or pulses you want, or a mixture is good, too, and you can play around with the pasta sauce as well. If you're coldy (and if no child is eating this), I suggest you use the spiciest, hottest sauce you can find.

While we're on the subject, let me just give you a quick outline of another fast soup, excellent for children's tea and much beloved *chez moi*. We call it easy *risi e bisi*, as it's a simplified version of the Venetian risotto-like soup that uses rice and peas, and here goes: put 1 litre of veg stock in a pan with 125g frozen peas, 300g risotto rice and 25g shaved, crumbled or grated cheese, let them come to a bubble and then simmer, with a lid on for 20 minutes. At the end, I have to admit that I remove the lid and stir in 2 x 113g jars of 100% pea babyfood (Beech Nut Tender Sweet Peas, to be precise) and then ladle into bowls with more cheese for any child who wants.

This one is even faster.

1 x 400g can mixed beans (sometimes sold as mixed bean salad) or other
   canned beans
300g tomato-based pasta sauce of your choice
750ml hot chicken or vegetable stock
100g ditalini or other soup pasta

1 Drain the beans and put them into a saucepan with the pasta sauce and hot stock.

2 Bring the pan to the boil and then add the ditalini, cooking according to the instructions on the packet.

3 Once the pasta is tender, switch off the pan, remove to a cool surface and let stand for 5–10 minutes if you can bear to wait. The pasta swells in the soup and everything just gets better.

Serves 2–3

Merguez with Halloumi and Flame-Roasted Peppers

This is a regular supper at Casa Lawson. I keep packets of halloumi cheese on perpetual standby in my fridge, and the peppers in jars in the cupboard. But you could always use a packet of frozen chargrilled peppers; they don't need thawing before going into the oven. Or, indeed, if you slice them thinly enough, you can use fresh bell peppers. Merguez is my spicy sausage of choice here, but chorizo has a longer fridge life, if that's a consideration. Anything you can buy vacuum-packed can only help here. So if you can't find merguez, don't worry, though a good internet source is Edwards of Conwy (www.edwardsofconwy.co.uk).

8 merguez or spicy sausages, approx. 340g total
1 x 250g block halloumi cheese
1 x 220g jar flame-roasted peppers
1 x 15ml tablespoon garlic oil

1 Preheat the oven to 220°C/gas mark 7. Put the sausages into a low-sided roasting tin (this makes the cooking time quicker).

2 Cut the halloumi into 5mm slices and lay them on and around the sausages in the tin.

3 Take the peppers out of the jar and strew them around the sausages and cheese, cutting them into smaller slices and pieces as you go, then drizzle the oil over.

4 Cook for 15–20 minutes, by which time the sausages should have browned and the cheese should have coloured in places.

Serves 4

CURRY IN A HURRY

This is such a favourite fallback of mine, I would never be without the staples to make it: coconut milk and green curry paste in the cupboard; various packages of green veg in the freezer. Of course, there are the other bits and pieces, too, but these are the basic ingredients. The chicken thigh fillets I buy as and when I need them.

If you want to make this with fresh vegetables rather than frozen, then up the water (keeping the amount of stock concentrate the same) and indeed I would double it to 500ml. But if using frozen – which is how I make this 99% of the time, and why it is a great storecupboard standby – I find it easier to use a cappuccino cup, or similar, and measure out 1^{1}/$_{2}$ cups of each frozen green veg rather than weigh it. The chicken comes in packets, so that just keeps everything simple and straightforward.

This is what to cook when you find out mid-afternoon that you've somehow acquired 6 people for dinner that evening.

2 x 15ml tablespoons wok oil
3 x 15ml tablespoons spring onions, finely chopped
3–4 x 15ml tablespoons green Thai curry paste
1kg chicken thigh fillets, cut into strips about 4 x 2cm
1 x 400ml can coconut milk
250ml boiling water

enough chicken stock concentrate or cube for 500ml water
1 x 15ml tablespoon fish sauce (nam pla)
185g frozen peas
200g frozen soya beans
150g frozen fine beans
3 x 15ml tablespoons fresh coriander, chopped

1 Heat the wok oil in a large saucepan that owns a lid, drop in the spring onions and cook, stirring for a minute or two, then add the curry paste.

2 Add the chicken pieces and keep turning over heat for 2 minutes, before adding the coconut milk, stock (i.e. the water plus stock concentrate or cube) and fish sauce, then the frozen peas and soya beans.

3 Simmer for 10 minutes, then add the frozen fine beans to the mix and cook for another 3–5 minutes.

4 Serve with rice or noodles, sprinkling the coriander over as you do so. Put out a plate of lime wedges for people to squeeze over as they eat.

Serves 6

MELLOW MEATBALLS

This recipe uses many of the same standby ingredients as the chicken Curry in a Hurry (see previous recipe), but tastes very different. I buy organic beef mini meatballs from the supermarket, which makes this extremely easy to put together, and there'd be nothing to stop you freezing them and cooking straight from frozen, if that helps. In which case, I'd just pop them in hot sauce and not attempt to brown them first.

Sure you can make your own meatballs, but so long as you're happy with the provenance of the meat (which is always, always important), don't beat yourself up about cutting out a stage, when you know everyone's going to be happy come suppertime. Likewise the packet of diced veg: once everything's swimming in its mellow sauce, no one is going to be asking questions.

It's just a case of making life easier on yourself; frankly, no one else is going to.

3 x 15ml tablespoons red curry paste
2 x 15ml tablespoons vegetable oil
40 organic mini-meatballs, approx.
   600g total
1/2 teaspoon ground cinnamon
1 teaspoon ground ginger
1 x 400ml can coconut milk
1 x 400g can chopped tomatoes

1 x 410g can chickpeas, drained
1 x 350g diced butternut squash and
   sweet potato (supermarket packet)
500ml chicken stock from concentrate
   or cube, or from a tub
2 x 15ml tablespoons honey
20g (approx.) fresh coriander, finely
   chopped

1   Heat the red curry paste and vegetable oil in a large wide pan; when it starts sizzling, add the meatballs, turning them in the red oily mixture.

2   Sprinkle the cinnamon and ginger over the meatballs and fry for a couple of minutes.

3   Add the coconut milk, chopped tomatoes and drained chickpeas. Stir in the diced butternut squash and sweet potato, then the stock and honey.

4   Bring to a boil and simmer for 20 minutes. Serve with rice and decorate each plate with some chopped coriander.

Serves 4–6

Sausages with Sauerkraut

The *Choucroute Garnie* I wrote about many years ago in *How to Eat* took several hours to make and involved much anointing with goose fat – and very good it was, too. Truth to tell, I don't believe this to be any less good, though you may be surprised to find it in a storecupboard section. But it makes sense: the sauerkraut is preserved in jars, and the sausages are smoked. I keep a supply in my deep freeze, but that's only because I order them online frozen (from Donald Russell, www.donaldrussell.com); when I buy smoked sausages from the deli, I let them live happily in the fridge.

It may seem extravagant to use a whole bottle of wine to cook this in, but you really can taste the difference. And don't buy plonk: it's the quality of the wine that leaves its note on this whole dish.

This is very, very good with a pan of plain steamed potatoes alongside, and really isn't any work at all.

1 x 936g jar sauerkraut, rinsed in cold water and drained	8 smoked sausages, cut into smaller lengths if wished
2 teaspoons juniper berries	1 x 75cl bottle Riesling wine
3 dried bay leaves	1 teaspoon white peppercorns

1　Preheat the oven to 200°C/gas mark 6. Cover the bottom of a small to medium roasting tin with the drained sauerkraut.

2　Add the juniper berries, bay leaves and sausages.

3　Pour in the wine and sprinkle the peppercorns over.

4　Bring the tin to a boil on top of the hob, then cover with foil and put in the oven to cook for 30 minutes. Serve with steamed potatoes, if you wish, and definitely some German beer mustard.

Serves 6

CHOCOLATE PEAR PUDDING

This is a cross between Pears Belle Hélène and Eve's Pudding, but the only important thing to remember is that this is easy, quick, very comforting and seems to please absolutely everyone. It's not hard to ensure you always have what you need in the house to make this. And, for hot days when baked sponge and sauce seems inappropriate, then bear in mind that canned (or bottled) pears and chocolate sauce – with or without vanilla ice cream – make a lovely pudding on their own.

You can make the Hot Chocolate Sauce on page 51, or buy one you like, obviously, but I have a complete storecupboard standby of a sauce which I make by heating together 1 x 170g can evaporated milk, $1/2$ teaspoon instant espresso powder, 150g golden syrup and 100g dark chocolate (minimum 70% cocoa solids).

The sponge itself does make a little bit of its own sauce, so if you really don't want to make some separately, just serve with chocolate ice cream.

As with any baking, you really do want to have all ingredients at room temperature before you start.

2 x 415g cans pear halves in juice	1 teaspoon baking powder
125g plain flour	$1/4$ teaspoon bicarbonate of soda
25g cocoa powder	2 eggs
125g caster sugar	2 teaspoons vanilla extract
150g soft butter, plus extra for greasing	

1 Preheat the oven to 200°C/gas mark 6 and grease a 22cm square ovenproof dish with butter.

2 Drain the pears and arrange them on the base of the dish.

3 Put all the remaining ingredients in a food processor and blitz until you have a batter with a soft dropping consistency.

4 Spread the brown batter over the pears, and bake in the oven for 30 minutes.

5 Let stand out of the oven for 5 or 10 minutes and then cut into slabs – I cut 2 down and 2 across to make 9 slices – and serve with chocolate sauce.

Serves 6–8

NUTELLA PANCAKES

Let joy be unconfined. This is one of the most irresistible puddings I think I have ever made, and I did it by no more than some fruitful scrimmaging about my cupboards. I long for it almost constantly, and it is not good that it is so easy to make, not good at all.

If you don't run to Frangelico yourself – and there is no reason why you should – then simply replace this hazelnut sticky liqueur with some rum. Incidentally, I love this as much when made with sweetened chestnut purée (though it's so strong, you could use much less) in place of the Nutella. In which case, I definitely use rum, and forgo the chopped hazelnuts, dotting with either a few crumbled marrons glacés as a special treat, or some chocolate sprinkles.

8 shop-bought crêpes	80ml Frangelico, plus 2 x 15ml tablespoons
1 x 400g jar Nutella	35g chopped hazelnuts (from a packet)
75g soft butter	250ml double cream

1 Preheat the oven to 200°C/gas mark 6.

2 Put each crêpe in front of you and spread some Nutella over one half, then fold the unspread side over the spread side. Now add a dollop of Nutella over one quarter and fold again, so what you have is a fat, squidgy fan. Place on a buttered swiss-roll tin or similar. Proceed with the remaining crêpes, overlapping them a little in the tin as you go.

3 Put the butter in a small pan with the 80ml Frangelico, and heat gently to melt.

4 Pour over the crêpes in their tin and sprinkle most of the chopped hazelnuts on top. Bake in the hot oven for 10 minutes.

5 Meanwhile, whisk the cream with the remaining 2 tablespoons Frangelico until you have an aerated soft floppiness, and put into a bowl, sprinkling with the last of the crushed hazelnuts. This luscious cream is a must alongside the sweet, buttery, heavenly crêpes.

Serves 6–8

CLAFOUTIS

A traditional clafoutis, from the Limousin region of France is, *tout court*, a baked custardy batter filled with cherries. The cherries, moreover, are not stoned, which I think has very little to commend it, save ease of execution. My version is even easier: I use stoned morello cherries (they must be sour to be a contrast to the sweet eggy batter) out of a jar, one or two of which are at all times to be found somewhere (usually the back) of my storecupboard.

Whereas the traditional Limousin pudding is baked slowly so that you have a soft, flan-like custard, I blitz mine brutally so it is more like a cherry-studded Yorkshire pudding. I've given the bare bones for my larder standby; but since I keep quite a crammed drinks cabinet, too, I often add 50ml Kirsch to mine, reducing the amount of milk to 250ml. The sweet-toothed might like to add 2 more tablespoons of caster sugar to counter the boozy hit, but I don't.

If you haven't got a tarte tatin dish to hand (I use mine for so many recipes, including roasting small birds, I can't recommend one too highly) use a 22cm pie dish or solid cake tin.

2 teaspoons vegetable oil	1 x 680g jar stoned morello cherries,
75g plain flour	drained to give 350g drained
50g caster sugar	cherries
4 eggs	1/2 teaspoon icing sugar (optional)
300ml semi-skimmed milk	

1 Put the oil in a copper tarte tatin dish or any shallow solid cake tin or pie dish of about 22cm diameter, then put the dish in the oven, preheating it to 220°C/gas mark 7 as you do so.

2 In a large bowl, mix the flour and sugar, then whisk in – either by hand or using an electric mixer – the eggs, one by one, the milk and the Kirsch, if using.

3 When the oven reaches the required temperature, stir the drained cherries into the batter, quickly open the oven, take out the hot dish and pour the cherried batter into it, popping the filled dish quickly back into the oven.

4 Bake for 30 minutes, by which time the sides will be bronzed and puffed, rising dramatically away from the edges of the tin, though it subsides pretty well immediately after it's come out of the oven, so the moment of pleasurable triumph is fleeting. Ah, well.

5 Let stand for about 10 minutes (20 is fine, and it is addictive cold, too) then dust with icing sugar just before serving, if the fancy takes you.

Serves 6–8

VANILLA APPLES WITH SWEETHEART CROÛTES

This is what I do when I am not expecting to make a pudding and have nothing much around and no time to be clever. I grab the apples from the fruit bowl – I've specified Gala, but use whatever's to hand – and take some slices of the children's plastic sliced white. And you know what? This really works. In an ideal world, I'd like a bit of thick pourable cream with, but if there isn't any, I'm not complaining.

50–75g butter

2 gala apples

2 x 15ml tablespoons vanilla extract

3 slices white bread, cut into heart shapes with a biscuit cutter

sugar for sprinkling

1   Melt the butter in a big pan, reserving a spoonful for later.

2   Finely slice the apples (don't bother to peel or core; curiously I get about 22 slices out of 2 apples, don't ask me how), and add them to the pan, cooking for about 3 minutes, then add the vanilla extract and cook for about another 5 minutes, turning once.

3   Remove the apple slices to a plate, then add the reserved spoonful of butter to the pan and quickly fry the sweetheart croûtes.

4   Arrange the sweetheart croûtes on the plate with the apples and sprinkle with sugar. Serve with cream if you've got some.

Serves 4

Acknowledgements

As I draw this book to an end, I conclude that I am extraordinarily fortunate in owing so many people thanks. The drawback is only that a long list requires an unwonted and unwarranted terseness. The china, linen, cutlery and general embellishment in the photos that precede this come from my own cupboards and an almost dangerous eBay habit, but on top of that I am grateful to the following: Absolute Flowers; Baileys; Cabbages & Roses; Ceramica Blue; The Cloth Shop; The Conran Shop; The Cross; David Mellor; The Dining Room Shop; Divertimenti; Gelateria Valerie; Habitat; Heals; Le Creuset; Liberty; OKA; Petersham Nurseries; The Pier; Something...; Summerill & Bishop; Thomas Goode.

I couldn't have produced these recipes without the food, delivered in almost comical amounts, by Allen's, James Knight, Michanicou Brothers and Panzer's.

Fiona Golfar, long-standing friend and überstylist, provided most of her furniture and also Rose Murray, my Second-Hand Rose, who in turn threw herself into the book, and my chaotic life, with charm and hard work, a winning combination.

I am grateful to Elinor Klivans and her publishers Chronicle Books, San Francisco, for permission to reprint her recipe for Totally Chocolate Chocolate Chip Cookies from her book *Big Fat Cookies*.

As ever, I am indebted, heartswellingly so, to Hettie Potter and Zoe Wales, my life-support system, who brought this baby into the world with me, as did Caz Hildebrand, whose instinct, wit, brilliance, unfailing eye and generosity are constantly invaluable to me. I am grateful to Francesca and Lisa Grillo, Anzelle Wasserman and Kate Bull for their support; without their work, I could not do my work. I feel extraordinarily blessed in my publishers, and want particularly to thank Poppy Hampson, Gail Rebuck, Alison Samuel, Will Schwalbe and Leslie Wells (and their backroom support teams, including Jan Bowmer and Mary Gibson). I am aware, too, of my good fortune in coming across Lis Parsons; her photographs provide just the pictures I dreamt of for my recipes.

It would be wrong, too, for me to fail to acknowledge my stepdaughter Phoebe, and my children Mimi and Bruno without whom this would be pointless.

To Ed Victor, my agent and friend, inordinate amounts of love: this is for you.

For Charles: thank you, thank you, thank you.

INDEX

INDEX